THE HIGH ACHIEVER'S
SECRET
CODEBOOK

THE UNWRITTEN RULES FOR SUCCESS AT WORK

BY SANDRA NAIMAN

D0521320

jist
Works
America's Career Publisher®

The High Achiever's Secret Codebook

© 2009 by Sandra Naiman

Published by JIST Works, an imprint of JIST Publishing
7321 Shadeland Station, Suite 200
Indianapolis, IN 46256-3923
Phone: 800-648-JIST   Fax: 877-454-7839   E-mail: info@jist.com

Visit our Web site at **www.jist.com** for information on JIST, free job search tips, tables of contents, sample pages, and ordering instructions for our many products!

Quantity discounts are available for JIST books. Have future editions of JIST books automatically delivered to you on publication through our convenient standing order program. Please call our Sales Department at 800-648-5478 for a free catalog and more information.

Trade Product Manager: Lori Cates Hand
Cover Designer: Zelen Communications
Interior Designer: Aleata Halbig
Proofreaders: Paula Lowell, Jeanne Clark
Indexer: Kelly D. Henthorne

Printed in the United States of America
14 13 12 11 10 09 9 8 7 6 5 4 3 2 1

    Library of Congress Cataloging-in-Publication Data
Naiman, Sandra M.
        The high achiever's secret codebook : the unwritten rules for success at work /
    by Sandra Naiman.
        p. cm.
  Includes index.
  ISBN 978-1-59357-622-6 (alk. paper)
1. Success in business. I. Title.
  HF5386.N323 2009
  650.1--dc22

                                                        2008050136

All rights reserved. No part of this book may be reproduced in any form or by any means, or stored in a database or retrieval system, without prior written permission of the publisher except in the case of brief quotations embodied in articles or reviews. Making copies of any part of this book for any purpose other than your own personal use is a violation of United States copyright laws. For permission requests, please contact the Copyright Clearance Center at www.copyright.com or (978) 750-8400.

We have been careful to provide accurate information in this book, but it is possible that errors and omissions have been introduced. Please consider this in making any career plans or other important decisions. Trust your own judgment above all else and in all things.

Trademarks: All brand names and product names used in this book are trade names, service marks, trademarks, or registered trademarks of their respective owners.

ISBN 978-1-59357-622-6

To my grandchildren: Becca, Taylor, Noah, and Julia

CONTENTS

PREFACE

This book was born out of my 20 years of experience as an executive coach and career consultant. I have worked with extremely successful professionals who attained considerable satisfaction and rewards from their work lives. I've also counseled others, just as capable and talented, who struggled and stumbled along their career paths.

Many who succeeded attribute their success to specific strategies or improvements that increased the company's profitability. Others refer to their work ethic and such things as "coming in early, staying late," "underpromising and overdelivering." Still others cite how they sacrificed: working weekends, losing sleep, and missing family time. And many say they were "just doing their job."

The obvious conclusion is that those who faltered along the way failed to abide by the same work habits and practices of those who did well. However, that is simply not the case. The fact is that those who somehow derailed themselves during the course of their careers seemed to be doing the same things as their counterparts. Yet they did not realize the same success. Why?

The answer does not lie with gender, amount of education, intelligence, or level in the organization. The distinction between the two groups is not due to tenure with the company or years in their profession.

The Secret Code for Success at Work

The critical factor that determines whether people make it into the winner's circle is *the way they conduct themselves daily* during the course of doing business. Although the winners certainly "play by the rules," they do something else. Those who succeed abide by simple, yet critical, codes of conduct—unwritten laws that mentors won't always teach and colleagues might neglect to mention.

Of course the workplace has a visible infrastructure with formal systems and processes. Without a doubt, company lore is full of plainly stated conventions guaranteed to lead to a corner office, vast resources, and a broad span of authority. But there is more. Every company has its own unique culture and covert standards that are equally if not more important to achieving success.

If these "off-the-record" rules go unheeded, seemingly harmless actions can pollute even the most promising of careers. This happens time and time again when good, hardworking employees, who are following the letter of the law, trip and fall over the unwritten codes with no clue as to where they went wrong.

When an unspoken law is broken, there is no immediate indication that anything is awry. The "guilty party" has no way of knowing that a rule has been breached. Hence, he or she will likely do it again. Over time, the repeated infractions add up, and a career seemingly on the rise suddenly heads south for no apparent reason.

Those who make it to the top in today's increasingly complex work world—and manage to stay there—have cracked the code and practice success secrets not available in employee handbooks or set forth in any values statement. They have learned to look beyond the obvious in order to interpret what is really going on in their work lives.

These high achievers very often do not even realize, nor can they articulate, the subtle differences that play such an important role in their success. Their habits either come so naturally, or have been acquired so imperceptibly that those who practice these success secrets do so without realizing it.

The Seven Secrets

This book sets forth these unspoken practices to help you accurately interpret the convoluted, not-as-it-seems-to-be corporate world. Although there is no formula or recipe that can be applied to every situation, there are strategies to decipher what is going on in your work life and select the most effective actions and responses. This book offers you a new pair of eyes and ears that will help you crack the code in each new situation you encounter.

The Introduction sets the context by examining basic needs and characteristics of people and describing how they play out in the work world. Each succeeding chapter closely examines a secret practiced by high achievers that helps them gain and maintain their career success. Those secrets are as follow:

+ **Secret 1—Tread Lightly:** This secret illustrates how, in a new situation, enthusiasm and the desire to make an immediate contribution can lead to recklessness that can permanently damage the relationship with a new team, boss, or company. You will learn how to slowly integrate yourself in a way that lays the groundwork for future success.

+ **Secret 2—Play Nice with Everyone:** This secret examines the many sources of influence within an organization, highlighting that power is not determined by title alone. You will learn how to assess the power structure in order to make things happen, and also to avoid the problems that result from miscalculating who does and does not have power and influence.

+ **Secret 3—Yield the Floor:** This secret advises that you let go of the idea of "right" and "wrong" and learn to make choices according to many different, and perhaps more critical, criteria. It teaches you to consider a variety of factors before taking a firm stand on any issue. You will learn that achieving consensus and winning cooperation are often more important than arriving at the "right" answer.

+ **Secret 4—Listen Between the Lines:** This secret addresses the issue of obtaining accurate and meaningful feedback. Your performance review does not necessarily reflect how you are really perceived by others in the organization. You will learn to be alert to indirect feedback and also gain skills in soliciting and graciously receiving direct feedback from others throughout the company.

+ **Secret 5—Get Over Yourself:** This secret cautions against overestimating your value and underestimating your vulnerability to mistakes and indiscretions. You will learn how easy it is, over time, to come to feel too safe, cross the line, and commit infractions that are not easily overlooked or forgiven.

+ **Secret 6—Blow Your Horn Softly:** This secret teaches you how to spread the word about your achievements and contributions without sounding like a braggart or blatant self-promoter. You will learn how to identify and create opportunities to talk about yourself and show what you can do in the natural flow of your work life conversations.

+ **Secret 7—Keep Sight of the Shore:** This final secret warns that there is a fine line between self-confidence and overconfidence and you will learn how to distinguish between the two.

Who This Book Is For

This book is not just for people who have stumbled in their careers and don't know why—those passed over for promotions, left out of the loop, or maybe even fired.

This book is for successful, talented, young professionals who appear to be rising stars. This book is for new and seasoned managers, and for valued contributors who continue to move up the ladder. This book is for ambitious people, new to the world of work, determined to make it big.

This book is also a reference for human resource and organizational development professionals as well as for executive coaches.

ACKNOWLEDGMENTS

There are many fine minds and committed people who contributed to this book coming to fruition and I am extremely grateful to all of them. My agent, Laurie Harper, has helped to grow this idea from its inception. She has spent countless hours brainstorming and advising me and I not only appreciate her wise counsel, but I also thank her for how much *fun* it is to work with her. My editor, Lori Cates Hand, and the other people at JIST Publishing have been delightful to work with and I acknowledge both their contributions and professionalism. Many friends and colleagues have given generously of their time to share ideas and provide feedback: Jean Gonzales, Sydelle Harms, Gail Hytner, Judy Pliner, Dana Smith, Jacquette Tara, and Sam Trenka. And I am blessed with many friends and family who have supported and encouraged me along the way. Thank you all.

CORPORATE RATIONALE IS AN OXYMORON

Organizations Aren't Always Driven by Logic

E verything that happens in the work world is not necessarily what it appears to be. It is a mistake to take it at face value. The corporate landscape is full of pitfalls and subtle intricacies. There are unseen forces rumbling beneath the ground that influence what happens on the surface.

If your expectations and decisions are based solely on what is obvious to you, the way things are supposed to work, or what makes sense, you will often be surprised and, sometimes, disappointed. Common sense often gets obscured as it works its way through organizational systems processes. It frequently emerges as something quite different than logic would predict.

Humans (and Their Organizations) Are Complicated and Unpredictable

Every organization has systems and policies designed to drive, measure, and reward individual and collective performance. These publicly stated practices and rules of conduct are clear-cut and absolute. However, there are many more that are unspoken and blurry; some might even run counter to the written rules. This is not due to intention, nor does it reflect a deliberate attempt to mislead people. Rather, it is simply due to the very nature of the beast.

People and the organizations they create are complicated. It takes time and due diligence to understand the subtle dynamics that can determine the difference between a stellar record and a career that gets derailed. Although written rules and regulations can be straightforward, the people who practice them are not. We humans are complex beings with predispositions that can make us unpredictable and seemingly unreasonable. Even though our brains have the capacity for logical and rational thinking, our human tendencies frequently drive us in the opposite direction. When you put a number of us together in an organizational setting, our "humanness" does not always align with systems and policies, nor is it openly acknowledged and sanctioned.

These human predispositions are much more transparent, and therefore easier to recognize, when we observe the behavior of children. Children want to get their way. When they don't, they will pitch a fit without regard to who might witness it. Children crave attention and they brazenly ask for it with such demands as "mommy, mommy look at me." Children love to win. They clap with triumphant glee when they do and pout inconsolably when they don't.

And guess what? We don't totally outgrow these needs. They are a part of our human nature. However, as we are growing up, we learn that we must share; we are told to be nice to everyone and that it is important to be a good loser. We are taught not to brag or gloat and we learn to control our emotions. But just because we learn to "act our age" does not necessarily mean that these tendencies are gone. Our behavior, at one time or another, to some degree or another, continues to be influenced by them.

Things to Keep in Mind About People

What follows is a brief discussion of the characteristics that are likely to shape how people perceive their circumstances and opt to behave in any given situation. As you review them, you might find yourself evaluating them as "good" or "bad," "wrong," or "different from the way things should be." Don't let such judgments get in the way of the usefulness of the information. This is not meant to imply that these tendencies motivate everybody all the time, but they do influence some people some of the time—and this includes you. So view the following discussion as a tool to help you to determine what might be going on under certain circumstances, especially when those circumstances run counter to logic.

People Want to Be Right

From our early learning experiences, adults cheer us on when we correctly name colors, recite the alphabet, and demonstrate mastery over our world. In school, we get gold stars, stickers, and A's for getting the right answers. We want to get as close as we can to 100 percent on tests and homework.

Somewhere along the way, we internalize the desire to be right, and it becomes its own reward. It just plain feels good inside to be right, and it is all the more delicious when other people witness and know about it.

Often in work situations and elsewhere, our discussions and debates are driven by this need to be right and it takes precedence over what might be best, or even over what is accurate. Because we do not live in a world that can be defined and understood strictly in terms of precise mathematical principles, these kinds of conversations can go on and on with the ultimate goal of each party being that of proving themselves "right."

People Want to Be Recognized and Rewarded

When we reach adulthood, instead of test scores and grades, we get raises and titles that recognize, acknowledge, and publicly signify that we have done the right things and found the correct answers. We have learned to expect tangible and intangible rewards for our "rightness." We want pats on the back, thanks, bonuses, and other perks that signify we have done well.

In a world that emphasizes prizes and awards, it is not surprising that the reward is seen as a validation of a job well done. At times, it is easy to focus more on the recognition than the end results of our efforts. It is almost as though our work does not stand on its own merits, and does not count until there is some public recognition of it. This is not necessarily true for everyone all the time, but it happens often enough to explain how certain situations play out in the workplace.

People Are Competitive

If humans are not born with a competitive gene, we certainly learn to value winning from a very early age. Our culture bombards us with all kinds of messages about the virtues of being number one. We learn to assess ourselves constantly in terms of how we compare with others. In an overtly competitive situation, we love how it feels to take first prize.

In the workplace, these prizes include awards, promotions, compensation, bonuses, and prestigious assignments. Because all of these are seen to be in limited supply, people naturally feel as if they are in competition with one another to achieve them. In games and sports, this rivalry is open and acknowledged by all involved. The rules are clear and accepted by each player, and they are applied equally.

By contrast, in the work world competition is not always overt, nor is it necessarily appropriate in all the situations where it surfaces.

A task force is formed for achieving a common goal, not for its members to jockey for position. A presentation is not supposed to be an opportunity to outshine a coworker. A conference call is not set up as a venue for someone to tout his or her latest and greatest accomplishment. However, we all know that these things happen. Further, competition often influences the way people assess a problem or situation, choose the actions to address it, and relate to one another in the process.

Because such competitions are not overtly sanctioned, when they occur, they are disguised as something else. Conversations are about what is best for the business, or the needs of a particular situation. There is absolutely no reference to the fact that competition between the players plays a role in the way they choose to define a situation and the actions they endorse to address it.

> *CAUTION: Although competition does frequently influence people's perceptions and behavior, it is a mistake to assume that it always does. There are different degrees to which competition drives behavior in any given situation. Furthermore, different people compete for different things, in different ways, at different times.*

People Are Territorial

Territoriality is a wired-in trait that begins in early childhood and never quite disappears. "Mine" is a word that children frequently attach to toys and other objects. When we reach adulthood, the word might not escape our lips quite as often, but it does continue to echo in our brains. Our sense of ownership applies not only to tangible objects. We also stake our claim to such things as job responsibilities, title, attention, and the perks that come with rewards and recognition. We feel a strong need to protect and defend what we believe is, or should be, ours.

In addition, once something belongs to us, we react badly if it's taken away. Once we feel ownership of something, we don't want to let go, and it is not easy for us to share. If we have been given sole leadership for a task or a project, we feel we've lost something if another is assigned to share the responsibility. If we've always planned the summer picnic, we react badly if someone else is selected to do it. If we've been the high-potential employee in our department, we do not like it when a bright, young star comes on the scene.

People Become the Roles They Play

When we meet someone new and they ask us what we do for a living, we will most likely reply "I am an accountant," or "I am an executive assistant." Notice that we do not say "this is the work I do," but we literally associate what we *do* with who we *are*. Thus our title or function takes on a far greater meaning than simply how we earn our livelihood. We define ourselves in terms of the work we do.

With this close identification with what we do comes the need to compete for it, guard it, and improve upon it, for example by striving for promotions and more responsibility. We have a sense of ownership of our roles and responsibilities; therefore, we strive to protect them.

However, protecting a role or job title is not an approved rationale for business-related decisions. No company openly condones actions designed to help someone maintain a sense of his or her own value, or feel secure in his or her job. No manager has permission to say "I don't want to create this new function because it threatens my own position." Therefore, other rationale will be put forth for such decisions that might or might not make the most sense, or even necessarily reflect what is in the best interests of the business.

People Want to Control Their Environment

People get a sense of well-being and security by having control over particular aspects of their lives. How much control and over what varies greatly from person to person, but most seek control over finances, health, career, and livelihood. When that sense of control is threatened, we will go to great lengths to regain it.

We achieve a sense of control over our work life in many ways. We gain new knowledge and skills to ensure that we remain valuable. We produce quality work and get recognized for it. We develop relationships inside and outside the company. We remain informed about what's going on in our company and our industry.

When circumstances or events lead us to fear a loss of control, we scramble to get it back. We might hoard information. Perhaps we work hard to call attention to ourselves or, conversely, fly under the radar. We might introduce or champion initiatives that require our particular skill set. There are as many ways to regain control as there are people. What we can be sure of is that the need for control will motivate behavior when the sense of it is threatened.

People Communicate in Euphemisms and on Many Levels

Our words represent only a small portion of the signals we use to communicate with others. We also convey information through our facial expressions, tone of voice, and body language. So often, our words send one message while our body sends another. There are innumerable opportunities for misunderstanding due to mixed messages and different meanings assigned to the same words.

The work world presents further opportunities for miscommunication because people don't always say exactly what they think. We develop one set of words that really mean something else. For example, one company might refer to major mistakes as "the learnings." In many situations "I think your suggestion is way off base," translates to "help me understand how you arrived at that."

About Organizations

Given the aforementioned tendencies of humans, let's examine how it plays out when you put a bunch of us together in any kind of structured system.

Different Perspectives Exist

Different people, at different levels, for different reasons, have different perspectives. Most situations, issues, and problems are open to many different interpretations. How a person reads a particular circumstance is an interaction of many factors, influenced by past, present, and future experiences, interests, needs, and desires. Often one person's version of a situation is likely to differ from another's. Once an individual arrives at his own interpretation of an issue or circumstance, it constitutes reality for him and there is a strong investment that it indeed represents the "truth."

Remember the parable of the six blind men feeling different parts of the elephant, and therefore coming to conflicting conclusions about how to describe it. Depending on what part of the animal he was feeling, one man described it as a wall, another like a spear, yet another like a snake, and so on. Likewise, different factions and different people come to perceive an organization and its issues from their own perspectives.

Unlike the world of math and science, there is no methodology to arrive at one right answer or ultimate truth in the world of work, and it's futile to even attempt to do so. Perception *is* reality; and usually, either power or majority rules in defining what that reality is. After reality is defined, when the party line is that the emperor is clad in beautiful colors made of the finest silks, no one has permission to even consider that "the emperor has no clothes."

Communication Channels and Information Flow Breed Inconsistencies and Misunderstandings

If a conversation between just two people that takes place face-to-face is subject to misinterpretation and misunderstanding, the chance for such confusion increases exponentially within an organization. When we add more people, more levels, more channels, more processes, and more protocol, it is virtually impossible for everyone to consistently operate from the same perspective, with the same information and understanding.

Organizational communication is further complicated by the fact that information is a precious commodity. Given the internal competition for power and influence, information becomes an important advantage, and often it is used for personal and professional gain. Some people hoard information. Some see it as a status symbol and use it to show that they are "in the know." Others use information to influence others and might put a spin on it to advance their own interests.

Generational Differences Impact the Workplace

At this writing, baby boomers (people born between 1946 and 1964) and generation Xers (born between 1965 and the late 1970s) make up the majority of the workforce. Of course, generation Y (born after the late 1970s) is rapidly growing in numbers. We are all a product of the times during which we grew up and it affects the way we perceive work, our basic values and work ethic, how we communicate, and what motivates us.

Although there are varying reports and studies as to how and how much these differences factor into our work lives, there is no denying that they do to some extent. Intergenerational differences add to the complexity of the work environment and make unraveling the dynamics all the more challenging.

Constant—and Sometimes Significant— Organizational Change Is Inevitable

The survival of any business depends on its ability to respond to its environment: the economy, the marketplace, technology, and so on. In a climate of ever-more-sophisticated technology and global competition, staying power requires constant, rapid, and often dramatic change. The bottom line is that anyone working in any size organization is required to maneuver in a world that might not be the same from one day to the next.

Cyberspace Is Rife with Opportunities for Misinterpretation

To amplify an already complex work environment, we cannot avoid, to a lesser or greater extent, the need to navigate through the virtual world. The business world is heavily dependent on cyberspace for information, communication, and interaction. Increasingly more virtual teams are made up of geographically distant members and managers.

Virtual reality is anything but. Dealing via cyberspace fails to provide critical information and immediate feedback that is vital to effective communication and the accurate assessment of a situation. Misinterpretations already occur face-to-face when people have the benefit of tone of voice, facial expressions, body language, and immediate feedback. When this data is lacking, misunderstanding is almost unavoidable.

Nature abhors a vacuum. In the absence of pertinent data, people tend to make things up. They bring into play numerous factors that have nothing to do with the actual content of the communication or situation. Thus, they assign meaning that may or may not be accurate. Quite often, it is not.

Everything Is Happening Faster

Today's business environment demands quick and efficient operations and responses. Everyone has to do more and do it faster; and they are often required to be available to do it 24/7. With laptops, cell phones, and Blackberries, there literally is no down time. Thus there is not sufficient time to think things through, overcome exhaustion, or manage emotional responses.

Further, DSL and broadband Internet connections have bred intolerance of anything that doesn't happen in a nanosecond. The expectation is that there will be instant and concise communications and responses. In this fast-paced and demanding work world, there is little patience with lengthy e-mails or voice-mail messages that drone on and on. There is an expectation that, with so very much to do and so little time to do it in, too many words are considered a waste of time. The luxury of elaboration or validation, especially during interactions in cyberspace, simply does not exist.

Everyone Is Operating Under Stress

Given the demands of work and family life, time pressure, and overload, stressed-out people are interacting daily with other stressed-out people. This means that at one time or another, for some time or another, people are at less than their best selves. Under such conditions, they are prone to misinterpret and over- or under-react to a situation or particular communication. They are not as sharp, effective, or efficient as they would be under less trying circumstances. They are often physically exhausted and mentally spent.

About How to Manage

I offer the preceding discussion to give you a realistic picture and appreciation of organizations and the people who work in them. Certainly everything isn't the case all of the time, and there are varying degrees to which these factors come into play. Knowing that these issues could be influencing what is happening in any given situation will help you decipher the complex facts of corporate life. As a result, you will be better equipped to successfully manage your career in the throes of it.

As you learn to interpret the not-so-obvious and ever-changing variables that are in play within your organization, your continuing success becomes more firmly rooted. You must be able to make an astute observation of others and an honest assessment of your own interests and needs in order to choose the best course of action as often as is humanly possible.

TREAD LIGHTLY

Learn Where the Quicksand Is Before Taking a Stroll on the Beach

In your enthusiasm to hit the ground running in a new situation, be careful not to allow your zeal to translate to actions that might eventually undermine you. Your success to some degree—and usually to a great extent—will depend on your ability to establish productive working relationships.

Stephen Covey, author of *The 7 Habits of Highly Effective People,* uses the analogy of a bank account to describe how relationships work. He cautions that you want to make more deposits than withdrawals and to be careful never to overdraw your account.

Whenever you find yourself in new relationships—with a new company, job, boss, or team—assume that your bank account with them is at zero. They have no direct information about you in this new role, so anything and everything you do looms large. Be absolutely sure that, in the beginning, you make only deposits.

Don't Start Off in the Wrong Direction

Because you don't yet know about expectations, how the work flows, how and what kind of information is communicated, who the influencers are, and how people relate, you are at risk of overdrawing your account before you have anything in it. Although you certainly need to contribute from the start, there are strategies to keep from going so far in the wrong direction that you cannot turn back.

Michael had been a network specialist at a large electronics manufacturing company for four years. He was elated to be selected to participate on a task force for a critical conversion. The project was highly visible throughout the company and under the close scrutiny of senior management. Michael thought he had finally gotten the opportunity to launch himself to stardom.

He made sure that he was ever-available to Karen, the project lead, and was constantly alert for the opportunity to become invaluable to her. Michael was always front-and-center and managed to get the plum assignments that would put him in front of senior management. Karen was delighted to have such an eager, capable resource and began to seek him out to take on more and more responsibility.

Michael's close collaboration with Karen meant less time working directly with his colleagues. She monopolized most of his workday, and Michael's exchanges with his coworkers were limited to relaying information and assignments from Karen.

Without warning, Karen was removed mid-project. Leadership was reassigned to one of his teammates; Michael found himself relegated to a lesser role.

On the face of it, Michael had done exactly as he should to make the most of this assignment to propel his career. He knew the importance of quickly establishing his value, and he demonstrated his competence and willingness to work from the first meeting of the task force. Michael consistently delivered on time, produced quality results, and got nothing but positive feedback. Based on what he saw and heard, he was off and running.

The problem was that he was off and running in the wrong direction! Michael was too quick out of the chute. He committed himself early to a plan of action that quickly picked up its own momentum. Even had he attempted it, he would not have been able to reverse his course.

While Michael thought he was making major headway and a valuable contribution, he was alienating the other team members. His colleagues resented his ambition and were distracted and demoralized by Karen's obvious dependence on him. Although Michael might have appeared to be a valued asset, he was actually a liability to the morale and effective functioning of the rest of the team.

Michael's negative impact on the task force came to the attention of senior management, who were highly invested in the success of the conversion. Rather than offer coaching to Karen, they decided on a more expeditious solution and replaced her with someone who had already earned the group's trust and respect. By appointing someone from the team, they hoped to encourage collaboration and benefit from the talent of all the members.

By the time this decision was made, Michael's fate was sealed. Because his peers regarded him as a "hot dog," "out only for himself," he was assigned tasks that would minimize his visibility and clout. And because he had alienated the others, there was no avenue for him to get the feedback he needed in order to correct his behavior in the future.

Consequently, he concluded that he would have to try even harder moving forward and he intensified his efforts to stand out and win the favor of those above him. His virtual demotion was apparent up and down the organization. "The word" was that he was difficult to work with; and indeed, his renewed efforts corroborated this perception.

Act as Though You Don't Yet Have the Job

When you're chosen for a new job, promotion, or task force, it is tempting to think that you have already won. Certainly, if you come with a history of past achievements, it can be an advantage. However, even if you have a strong track record and your reputation precedes you, you cannot assume that you are firmly established in a new situation. And often, quite the opposite is true.

Your performance in your new role reflects on the competence of those who selected you. You can be sure that they are closely observing you to confirm that they made a good decision. Find out why you were chosen and plan your projects and priorities to showcase what they perceived to be your strengths.

You can also assume that everyone with whom you are working is watching you. And, the higher and more influential your position, the more scrutiny you will be under. The most prudent approach when in a new role is to behave as though you are still vying for it. Conduct yourself as though you have yet to win the confidence and approval of the stakeholders. Indeed, that is quite likely the case.

Action Items

❑ Confirm with the decision maker(s) why you were selected for a job, promotion, or special project.

❑ List opportunities to demonstrate the strengths, traits, and talents for which you were selected.

Learn the "MO" of the Team

Individuals and teams develop habits, preferences, and expectations about the way they interact with one another and how work is accomplished. If the team has a prior history together, you can avoid unnecessary withdrawals from your account if you adapt quickly to their way of doing things.

When a team comes together for the first time, have discussions about people's work and communication preferences. Explore what is important to team members in terms of how they find satisfaction in their work. Ask them how they feel they can make a meaningful contribution. Find out what each considers his or her strengths and weaknesses. Learn what you can do to support each member and what you might do that he or she would find detrimental or less than helpful.

If you are joining an intact team or department, be an astute observer of how the team goes about getting things done.

Communicate with the Boss

Start with your boss:

+ How does he or she prefer to communicate: e-mail, voice mail, or face to face?

+ Do you need to schedule meeting times or are "drop-ins" okay?

+ How does he or she feel about receiving cell phone calls? Can you call him or her about any situation or only in emergencies?

+ Does he or she want to be contacted during evenings or weekends, and under what circumstances?

Observe the Team

Observe how your peers communicate with one another—how often and about what:

+ Who gets included and copied on e-mails?

+ How do they determine priorities and what are they?

+ Are decisions made collaboratively or from the top down?

+ Do they prefer to work in teams or independently?

+ What is the protocol at meetings or on conference calls—formal or informal?

+ Does a deadline mean at the eleventh hour or two days before?

+ What are the accepted topics for personal conversations?

Get the Backstory

If you come in as a manager, before you officially assume your new role, find out as much as you can from your boss:

+ Ask whether any of your direct reports wanted the position. If so, what happened and what is the best way of working with him or her?

+ Are there any special circumstances you should know about?

+ What was your predecessor's management style?

+ Were people glad or unhappy to see him or her leave?

Win Over Your Direct Reports

Remember that your direct reports are essential to your success and can provide you with valuable information and support in your new role. If you are taking over an intact team, acknowledge the value of the way they are accustomed to doing things.

On your first day, hold a meeting with your entire team. Introduce yourself and enlist their help in learning the organization and its people. Let them know your schedule and that you look forward to meeting with them individually. Offer them the opportunity to ask questions.

Refrain from sharing your mission, expectations, or how you might change things. This meeting is to make them comfortable with you. During individual follow-up meetings, ask them how they are used to being managed and what kind of support they need from you. Again, don't discuss any changes you intend to make or offer opinions on how things could be done better. Make only favorable observations and comments. Do let them know about your style and preferences so that you can negotiate these new relationships rather than dictate them.

Virtual Alert

If you are managing people at different locations and your budget permits, bring them together face-to-face as soon as possible. Plan a meeting off-site to cover business issues, go on group social outings, and have one-on-one meetings with your direct reports.

After that, schedule regular conference calls. Make sure the agenda is constructive and clear and that you adhere to time frames. Choose to talk to your direct reports over the phone when appropriate, instead of relying exclusively on e-mail. Make a point to visit each of their sites as the budget and your schedule allow. Don't forget to engage your boss so that he or she supports the use of your time and the travel expenses.

Action Items

☐ Schedule a meeting with the boss or lead to explore how he or she prefers to manage.

☐ Make a list of coworkers and check with each about her or his work habits and preferences.

☐ Schedule meetings with direct reports as a group and individually.

☐ Record preferences and review regularly to ensure that you honor them.

Ask the Right Questions

When you are new, there is much that you do not know: how the department functions, its history, what works and what doesn't, what is looked upon favorably, and what might be taboo. Asking the right questions is as important, or even more so, than having the right answers. Asking questions of your boss, peers, and direct reports will accelerate your learning curve. And just as important, you are demonstrating your interest in them and your respect for their experiences and viewpoints.

You can expect others to welcome your inquiries as long as the questions are genuine, well-thought out, and don't use an inordinate amount of their time. Find out as much as you can on your own before approaching others. Then you can ask the in-depth questions that will show that you did your homework.

Compile a list of questions and ask someone to lunch or set an appointment with the express purpose of learning from them. On a more informal basis, as you are working with others in the course of the business day, be alert to opportunities to ask questions. Listen carefully and do not be too quick to jump in with your own ideas before you have heard theirs.

Until you have a well-grounded understanding of how things are done and what is important to whom, it is best to be circumspect about introducing new ways of doing things or challenging someone else's ideas or opinions. That is not to say that you should totally refrain from sharing your thoughts or making suggestions. Just be sensitive in doing so and choose carefully, so that it doesn't seem like you want to overhaul everything.

When you do offer your ideas, refrain from referring to other teams or other companies. You don't want to sound like you are living in the past or tied to only one certain perspective or approach. Nothing can get older or more annoying to the ears than the phrases "when I was with…" or "the way we used to…."

When you want to introduce a new idea, start out by asking questions and offering your perspective carefully and noncritically. Use questions such as "Have you ever considered eliminating this step?"; or "What do you think would happen if we waited until after we got feedback from the client before we ran the idea by marketing?" If you get pushback, weigh the potential pros and cons of persistence.

Even if you are absolutely positive that you have the right answer—and even if you are the boss—you are at risk of losing more than you stand to gain by coming on too strong to push your point of view. You don't want to step on sacred cows, be seen as unreceptive, or come across as a know-it-all.

Ignore These Thoughts!

If you find these thoughts running through your mind, don't listen to them!

- ✦ "I know once they try it this way, they'll like it better."
- ✦ "I wasn't hired to be a yes person."
- ✦ "Once they understand my reasoning, they're sure to see things my way."

Avoid Asking Taboo Questions

Taboo topics are particularly difficult to discover because people don't talk about the things they don't talk about. So it's tricky to know what those are until you step in one.

When you are in a new situation, pay attention not only to what kinds of things people do talk about, but also what they don't. As much as possible, confine your comments and suggestions to those subjects that, by observation, you have assured yourself are open ones.

Sometimes you can identify the taboo topics because they are as obvious as the emperor not wearing any clothes. For example, a project is fossilized, counterproductive, and a drain on resources, yet no one is addressing it. It's a good bet that questioning this undertaking is taboo. You can assume that when something is obvious to you, it is probably obvious to others as well. Therefore, when it never comes up in meeting or cubicle conversation, it is best to conclude that it is forbidden.

Even for those subjects that are open, you need to be careful of asking too many "why" questions, such as "why do you always double-check with the customer before reissuing a standard order?" You might genuinely be interested in learning the logic behind something or understanding the process of how decisions get made. However, asking too many "why" questions could be interpreted as your way of critiquing standard and accepted practices.

> *Pete was a newly hired foreman for a commercial construction company. He was overseeing a large development project for an oil corporation moving to the state, promising thousands of new jobs. Construction was running way behind schedule and there was considerable pressure from all sides. The delays were being attributed to bad weather and equipment snafus. During a lengthy discussion about the delays at a project review meeting, Pete felt he could easily see the problem and could not restrain himself any longer.*
>
> *"Excuse me, I have a question," he said. "I was wondering why we don't just switch cement contractors? They have been slowing us down from the beginning and don't show any signs that they care at all."*
>
> *The room went silent. Pete had suggested what everyone was thinking, but what no one dared mention.*

Pete had violated a taboo—a cultural agreement not to engage in a discussion about a particular topic. A topic of conversation can be open, restricted, or off-limits. When there is mutual agreement to talk about a topic, it is an open one. If one person is willing but the other is not, the topic is restricted. If both parties are unwilling, the topic is off-limits. When everyone agrees that a topic is off-limits, it is most likely taboo.

Engage All the Stakeholders

When you assume a new position, enlist the support of people who have a vested interest in and will be affected by what you do. This includes, of course, your boss, peers, and direct reports. It also consists of anyone else inside and outside the company who can approve, block, or influence decisions, and those in a position to champion or derail your efforts.

Talk to these people. Show your interest in them. Ask them about their challenges. Find out what they need from you. Seek to understand what constitutes a "win" for them, and what makes them look good in the organization. Then be alert to opportunities to support them.

Offer to help a colleague compile a vital report. Pitch in when your direct reports are in a time crunch. Ask your boss how you can help her or him prepare for an important presentation. Acknowledge the heavy workload of administrative staff and ask how much lead time they need to complete work for you. The more you demonstrate responsiveness and support toward others, the more likely they will offer the same to you.

> *Sharon was promoted from southwest regional sales manager for a financial products company to district manager for the eastern United States. The southwest had a strong sales team and Sharon had enjoyed considerable success in her regional role. Her strength was market analysis and she was promoted with a mandate to increase revenues by penetrating new markets.*
>
> *The previous district manager had been very "hands on" rather than strategic, which was the primary reason he had been replaced in that role. He held too many meetings with his direct reports and their staffs, tracked activities constantly, and provided frequent direction and feedback.*
>
> *After moving to New York and scheduling "getting to know you" visits with the field, Sharon set up weekly conference calls with the regional managers and tracked activity through the usual reporting systems, careful to monitor sales and ensure they were holding steady while she set about fulfilling her charge.*

(CONTINUED)

(CONTINUED)

> She quickly focused on gathering data and researching the demo-
> graphics to identify opportunities to move into new markets. Sharon
> correctly assessed the need to manage across and up, and she worked
> hard to develop collaborative relationships with colleagues and credi-
> bility with her boss and the senior team.

> Sharon's peers were supportive and closely observed her methods and
> processes, hoping to replicate her efforts in their own territories. When
> it came time to introduce and implement her strategy, the plan was
> well received and strongly endorsed by senior management. However,
> when it was rolled out to the field, the expected results simply were
> not realized.

> Sharon visited each of the field offices to hear what she considered to
> be excuses rather than real problems and roadblocks. However, she
> was unable to overcome resistance and produce the ambitious goals
> she had promised.

Sharon's undoing was her failure to involve vital stakeholders—her
direct reports and their sales staffs. The field was accustomed to more
attention from the district manager and her style was interpreted as self-
serving and unsupportive. She neglected to involve and keep them
apprised of her efforts. People in the field felt dismissed and devalued.

Consequently, Sharon's plan was greeted with under-enthusiasm and
silently sabotaged by the people who had to implement it. When she
sought feedback in order to provide people in the field with the support
necessary to make the plan successful, it was too late for her to redeem
herself.

Virtual Alert

When you are dealing with people at a distance, engaging the
stakeholders is just as important but a bit trickier to accomplish. Your efforts have to be more deliberate in that you will

not be presented with the kind of ad hoc encounters that allow you to informally engage others and learn more about them. If you have some stakeholders at a distance and others "just down the hall," be especially careful not to engage or rely on the latter more heavily because of their proximity. You need to go to extra lengths to make sure that everyone feels acknowledged, valued, and "in the loop."

If you are charged with the execution of a specific project, identify the key stakeholders. Determine who might want to undermine, derail, or sabotage the project; who might be able to prevent that; who you need as a champion; who can help achieve a successful outcome; and who the key influencers are. Plan and implement a strategy to approach and engage these people. The more time you spend building goodwill with each of them upfront, the more you will be able to count on their support as you move forward.

Action Items

❏ Identify and create a file for each stakeholder.

❏ Record what they need from you, their goals, and their "wins."

❏ Note anything you can do to support them.

Secure Early Wins

When you are yet unproven in a new role, a couple of homeruns coming out of the box can be of great value in establishing your expertise and ability to do the job. Assume that your boss wants you to succeed and ask him or her to help you identify two or three things you can achieve early to make a visible and valued contribution.

Be sure to clarify time frames, resources available, expected outcomes, and how success will be measured. Ask what has been tried before; what worked and what didn't. Explore any potential organizational roadblocks and identify the key supporters and stakeholders.

Irene was promoted to director of production for a leading manufac-turer of automotive parts. Inventory management was a major issue, spiking production costs and impacting delivery to customers. Irene tackled this problem almost immediately and made it a number-one priority.

She was careful to get buy-in from all the stakeholders: her boss and colleagues, and all the way to the people on the manufacturing floor. She kept everyone informed of progress and snags, and sought fre-quent feedback in order to facilitate a solution.

The sources of the problem were quite complex and Irene ran into many dead ends on her way to correcting it. She continually had to involve other departments and win over new players. Eventually, management lost confidence in her ability to effectively solve the prob-lem and a cross-functional task force was created to address it. They picked up where Irene left off and successfully resolved the inventory-management issues within three months.

Irene made no major errors in her attempt to revamp the inventory-management system. Due to corporate culture, politics, and the com-plexity of the problem, the process would have been a long one no matter who was at the helm. The rapid success of the task force was the result of all that Irene had accomplished prior to its formation.

Irene's mistake was that she failed to establish her competence before undertaking such a difficult and long-term project. Essentially, she didn't have enough in her bank account as director to cover the with-drawals that resulted from the lengthy course of the project.

Irene should have identified some early, more easily achievable wins before going into battle against such an unwieldy beast. She needed to establish her ability to get things done so that others would not lose faith in her when she ran into inevitable glitches in solving the inventory-management problem.

Virtual Alert

When your wins might not be readily apparent to people at a distance, you will want to bring them to their attention. Be careful to do so in a way that is not misinterpreted as self-promoting. Remember, you have very little in your bank account.

You might be able to mention your plan at the inception of the undertaking when referring to your schedule or daily activities. If the outcome impacts others, it makes sense to let them know how their lives will be easier or different. Also by getting the input of others, you can make them aware of what you are doing without appearing pretentious.

Ask for Guidance and Feedback

From the beginning, you want to be vigilant to ensure that you get on—and stay on—the right track. Set clear, measurable goals with benchmarks along the way to make sure you are going in the right direction. Some metrics are objective and speak for themselves, such as sales goals, timeliness, and cost savings.

Others, however, require input from others. The only way you can be sure you are on the right track where quality and style issues are concerned is to ask. It is important that you do just that, and do it often. The key is in knowing what to ask and who to ask.

When you are new to a group, selecting who to seek out for guidance and feedback can be a bit tricky. If you are so fortunate as to have developed a solid relationship with someone in the group prior to joining it, he or she could be a perfect resource.

If this is not the case, you are in the position of turning to people with whom you have very little in your bank account. Therefore, you need to follow certain guidelines in order to avoid appearing incapable or unsure of yourself, making the person you are asking feel uncomfortable, or discouraging valuable feedback in the future.

Ask from a Position of Strength

You have been selected to do a particular job because you are expected to be qualified and skilled at it. You want to get the vital input and feedback to ensure your success without giving the impression that you are not up to the job.

To do so, make sure that you do your homework and learn everything you can on your own. If you are giving a presentation or report, ask to see others that were successful in the past and learn from them. When you ask for input on your efforts, be sure that it reflects the best of what you can do on your own without feedback from anyone. You always want to do as much as you possibly can by yourself before asking another to help you improve on it. You want your boss or colleague to feel as though his or her task is to make something good better, rather than to fix something that is deficient.

Carefully Select Your Sources

Later in the book, Secret 4 advises that when you voluntarily solicit feedback, whether or not you act on it is a choice. This is true after you have a solid bank account, but it is not the case when you are in a new situation. Because you have not yet established your receptivity and appreciation of feedback, this is the time that you must do so.

If you request someone's input or feedback and fail to take action on it, he or she can easily conclude that you didn't really want it in the first place and to provide it was a waste of time. Further, in the absence of a history that says otherwise, the person might decide that you have little regard for what he or she thinks. No matter how profuse your words of appreciation, the ultimate reward to anyone offering feedback is to see you do something in response to it.

Be careful that you have enough confidence in those you ask to act on the input they give you. If you are asking for input on a presentation, go to someone with effective presentation skills. If you are seeking advice on a technical issue, request input from someone who you know to be a subject-matter expert.

Do not ask for input or feedback on anything that you are unwilling to act on. If you are sure that you are on the right track or have the best answer for something, don't ask for someone else's opinion on the matter. Under such circumstances, you are really asking for validation and confirmation, fully expecting the other person to see things as you do. This is actually asking for validation, not requesting feedback. Be careful not to get the two confused.

Secret 4 goes into great detail about asking for feedback, but there are important points to also be considered here.

Be Clear About What You Want

A good way to ensure that you can act on the feedback and input of another is to be very specific about what you want to hear from them. Avoid broad requests such as "I'd like to get your input on my report." This leaves you open to getting suggestions based on another's own idiosyncrasies and style preferences, and those are often awkward to act on.

Instead, be clear about just what you want them to react to: "Is the introduction clear and succinct?" "Do you think there's too much information on such and such?" This ensures that you don't get information you don't want or can't use, and that you can actually act on the feedback you are given.

If you can anticipate a particular situation, choose someone ahead of time and direct her or his attention to the kind of information you are seeking. For example, prior to a meeting, you can ask someone for feedback on what you do or do not do to encourage others to participate, or if you demonstrate calmness in handling a volatile issue.

Action Items

❏ Identify situations and specifics for which you would like feedback.

❏ Identify and approach the individual(s) in a position to give you that feedback.

After receiving feedback, ask questions for clarification until you are sure you have understood the message and can take action on it. If the feedback indicated something was off or lacking, ask exactly what could have been better, different, or more helpful. If the feedback is glowing, ask questions that enlighten you as to exactly what you did right.

Remember that the purpose of soliciting feedback is not to make you feel good, but to ensure that you are heading in the right direction and staying on course. To this end, it is essential that people feel comfortable telling you what they really think. It's up to you to make sure that they do by the manner in which you react to their input.

Never retaliate or argue with feedback! The other person is telling you the truth as he or she sees it, so there really is no right or wrong insofar as feedback is concerned. To negate or debate will discourage someone from offering their thoughts in the future. There is nothing more critical to your success than getting honest opinions and feedback from others. From the very beginning, you want to make sure that they will be comfortable providing you with it.

Ignore These Thoughts!

If you find these thoughts running through your mind, don't listen to them!

✦ "Maxine won't think I came on too strong once I make it clear why I said what I did."

+ "Allen is wrong. I wasn't nervous during the presentation and I will tell him that I always shift from one foot to the other."

+ "If Sally knew how important this was to my success here, she would understand why I'm looking over everyone's shoulders. I know she'll agree with me once I explain."

Be Careful What You Reveal

If you have concerns about your abilities, second thoughts about your new role, or doubt about a decision your boss has made, keep it to yourself. Don't talk about run-ins with past colleagues, previous mistakes, or any other information that can be misunderstood or misinterpreted. If you must talk about such things, do so only with trusted friends outside the organization.

Share only benign information about your personal life—for example, married or single, children or none, hobbies and pastimes, favorite foods, and so on. You *do* want people to have a sense of you as a person in order to build good working relationships. However, you must avoid raising eyebrows or drawing people into your private life beyond where they are comfortable. Go very slowly in determining what kinds of topics are appropriate and what constitutes "too much information."

As a general rule, when in doubt—don't. Some subjects are best left at home no matter how high you are on the org chart or how long you've been with the company. Even if others engage you in discussions about their highly personal or sensitive topics, you are best served by avoiding the temptation to do the same thing. This might seem so patently obvious that it need not be mentioned. But be careful. It's easy to get so comfortable and confident that you get caught off guard and end up revealing things that you will later come to regret.

Stan had recently been promoted to CEO of an international engineering consulting company. His predecessor had opted for early retirement amidst rumors that the company was being positioned to be sold. Stan had been with the company for more than 10 years and he was regarded as highly charismatic, charming, and down-to-earth. He had strong relationships with the managers of the field offices and a reputation for being sincere and easy to talk to. His professional image was one of strength and self-assurance and he was able to influence both up and down.

Even though the parent company had assured him they had no intention of selling, he was not convinced they were being truthful and Stan was offended by their lack of disclosure. During his first meeting as CEO with field managers worldwide, he was constantly quizzed about rumors of the sale. During an informal gathering with a few of the managers whom he considered especially close, he commented: "I don't think they're telling me everything." He trusted that their previous relationship would permit this level of confidence.

Unfortunately, that did not prove to be the case. It was not long before the phone lines were buzzing around the globe. Not only did Stan's words spread like wildfire inside and outside the company, but because he allowed himself to show the chink in his armor, his credibility as a strong leader was irreparably impaired. In spite of fervent efforts at damage control, highly valued and talented people began to exit the company.

Stan mistakenly felt he could trade on his past performance and relationships without damaging his image. However, these managers had no experience with him in his new role; plus, they were anxious about their own jobs. Stan's sterling reputation and past achievements notwithstanding, his bank account as a CEO was empty.

By revealing his own misgivings, Stan increased the managers' apprehension and, by way of the grapevine, that of the rest of the company. His openness was perceived as a weakness and a detriment to his ability to lead. An off-the-record comment that would have been held confidential after he had established himself as a capable CEO caused significant and permanent damage.

Ignore These Thoughts!

If you find these thoughts running through your mind, don't listen to them!

+ "Certainly since Sally told me all about her ugly divorce, I can tell her about my domestic problems."

+ "Jack seems so supportive, I can tell him that I'm afraid this new job is way over my head."

+ "This project is going so well, it won't matter if I tell my coworkers that the team leader is driving me crazy."

Be Wary of E-mail

E-mail is fraught with opportunities for misinterpretation and unintended consequences. There are poisons in cyberspace that can contaminate and distort any communication passing through it. This is always the case—and even more so when it is your primary means of communication with people whom you do not yet know.

There are, however, practices that minimize the potential threats. Although it might take a little more time and thought, it's wise to take certain precautions before you click the Send button.

Assume Your Message Will Be Read Quickly

Business e-mail has become a medium of stress, often the courier of a multitude of tasks that make overwhelming demands on our time. People open their e-mail each morning with a sense of dread to learn just how frantic their day will be. They get through their messages as quickly as possible, meaning that they might miss subtleties and details.

Compose your messages carefully, including only necessary information. Don't ramble. Get to the point as quickly and briefly as possible. Stick to the subject matter of the e-mail. If you want to address a different issue, compose a new message. A long e-mail is not likely to be pored over word for word; thus, the reader might not notice important information or a change of subject.

> *CAUTION:*   *Be careful that your e-mail messages are not too brief. "Brief" can be synonymous with "brusque." When people know you more from your e-mails than from interpersonal contact, it is easy to create the impression that you are abrupt and impersonal. Even when they do know you well, there is the risk that the brevity will be misinterpreted, depending on the sensitivity around the subject of the message.*

Don't Disregard Business Protocol

Brevity need not translate to starkness. Although e-mail is certainly less formal than a business letter, the best practice is to always include a salutation and closing. Even if others don't respond in kind, it will never hurt you to follow some protocol. Perhaps rather than "Dear Sara," you want to say "Hi Sara," but some such introduction is more personal and personable than plunging into the content.

You might want to include a line—not content related—that addresses a prior contact or demonstrates an interest in the recipient. A reference to rain in their region or the victory of a sports team does not add inordinate length to your message, and it serves to build and maintain a positive relationship.

The "Feeling Factor" Creates Misunderstandings and Misinterpretations

An e-mail can announce a meeting time and agenda, request the status of a project, or contain some other such benign and straightforward communication. On the other hand, an e mail message can address an issue that is highly sensitive, about which people are likely to have strong feelings. This continuum, from the relay of uncomplicated information to the tackling of delicate issues, is what I call the Feeling Factor.

The Feeling Factor is predictive of the potential danger of any communication in the same way the Richter Scale can be indicative of the devastation from an earthquake. The higher the Feeling Factor, the more the potential for damage. Although this holds true for face-to-face and telephone conversations, it is off the charts for exchanges conducted through cyberspace.

Before you even consider broaching an issue via e-mail, take into account where it rates in terms the Feeling Factor. Examples of topics that should raise a red flag are the following:

+ You have to tell people that something did not go as planned or that you will be unable to follow through on something.

+ The recipient might see the message as critical of him or her.

+ The issues are heated and others have strong opinions or a vested interest in the outcome.

+ You have to take away something previously granted, such as an assignment to a special task force or resources committed to project.

+ You want to resolve a dispute or misunderstanding.

+ The message constitutes bad news about which the recipient will probably be disappointed or angry.

If your communication has a high potential Feeling Factor, consider a telephone or face-to-face conversation about the subject. If that is possible and practical, it would probably be the most prudent course of action.

> *CAUTION:* Be careful to initiate person-to-person contact only when it is warranted. With colleagues and clients under time pressure, you do not want to intrude on their concentration and other work with unnecessary phone calls or meetings when an e-mail could suffice.

Check Your Own Feelings

If you get an e-mail that sets off your feelings, don't react in the moment. Fingers flying across the keyboard in response are apt to send a message that you will come to regret.

Before taking any action, step away and calm down. Then reread the message in case there's any chance that you misinterpreted or perhaps overreacted. If you still have the same perspective, it is best not to reply by e-mail unless you stick strictly to relaying straight information. If you decide that you can do so and reply without animosity, have someone read your message before sending it to be sure that there isn't some hint of hard feelings lurking between the lines. Any retaliatory or defensive tone will serve only to exacerbate the situation. Cyberspace is absolutely not the arena for resolving disputes that involve anyone's emotions.

If you choose to talk to the sender in person or on the phone, be sure you are calm when you contact them. Do so not to get even, but to resolve the situation. And the first step is to validate your impression of the original message. It is quite possible that you misunderstood or misinterpreted. You certainly don't want to create a conflict where none existed.

Proofread...and Then Proofread Again

If all or most of your contact with a new person—or new people—is via e-mail, you are at an even greater risk of making a premature withdrawal from your account. You do not have the benefit of the immediate feedback available during telephone or face-to-face contact. Be very careful how you word your messages! Read and reread e-mails for anything that could be misinterpreted.

Your writing and writing style become part of who you are. Sending a message that contains typos or grammatical errors is tantamount to showing up for work in your bathrobe or meeting a client with a stain on your shirt. It will never serve you to come across as sloppy or unprofessional.

Learn the Protocol for Who Gets Copied

Because who has what information and why they have it is an important issue, who gets e-mails and who does not is also significant. Information is a source of power and an indicator of value and status. E-mails are also ways of documenting accountability. Thus, who you send a message to makes you subject to errors of omission and commission.

Copying someone's boss on an e-mail can be interpreted as holding his or her feet to the fire, or as a self-protection effort. Failing to copy the boss on the same e-mail could also be a violation of protocol. If you blind-copy someone, they could interpret this to mean that you are keeping something from the designated recipient. For all these reasons, be sure you understand the common practices and expectations so that you do not give off the wrong first impressions of how you do business.

Manage Expectations from the Beginning

You want to be seen as a team player, someone who will "do whatever it takes." So, when you are asked at the last minute to travel on Sunday for an early-morning meeting on Monday, you say yes. Of course you can move up the deadline and have your presentation ready a week early. Why not take on a coworker's project when she is called away on a family emergency? The next thing you know, it is assumed that you will respond in the affirmative to all such requests. It is all too easy to go from making an exception, under what feels like unique circumstances, to setting a precedent.

Indeed it can advance your career to go the extra mile and it is a good idea to do so. Just make sure it's a trip you want to take, and that you know exactly how far you are willing to go. Make the decision upfront and manage expectations all along the way.

Once the expectation is set, it is extremely difficult, if not impossible, to reverse. When you first attempt to do so, you will be forgiven with assumptions such as "she must be having a bad day," or "nobody can be perfect all the time." If it continues, however, others will eventually conclude either that they were wrong about you in the first place, or that you have changed and are not as cooperative as you used to be. They could even come to believe that now that you've made it, you don't feel that you have to work as hard, or that your success has gone to your head.

Once others come to expect certain behaviors or results from you, and, in their perception, you fail to deliver, the gap is huge and the contrast dramatic. And once that occurs, your bank account does not go just to zero. You are permanently overdrawn.

> *Mary was a technical whiz for a software consulting firm. Early on with the company she was recognized for her outstanding ability to design creative, cost-effective solutions and applications. Her colleagues constantly sought her out for advice and support because they were well aware of her exceptional skills.*

> *Mary was delighted to be seen as so competent. She welcomed and was quick to respond to her colleagues' requests. Soon they came to expect such generosity and to rely on her expertise to help them address challenging situations. Eventually, however, as her reputation spread, the situation got out of hand. She was putting in excessive hours in order to meet both client demands and her colleagues' needs. She continued to work excessively long hours but became more and more tired and stressed. When she asked to be relieved of some of her client load, she was told it was not an option.*

> *Thinking she was buffered by the goodwill she had previously earned, she became quite open about her workload being impossible and out of control.*

But by that time, Mary had established the expectation that she would act as an internal resource and there was no avenue by which she could reverse it. Her explanations of "too busy" or "no time" were simply not well received.

Although her colleagues' requests waned and they eventually came to stop relying on her, Mary's once-stellar reputation had morphed into one of "not a team player" and "too full of herself."

Mary needed to manage expectations from the beginning. Had she anticipated the demand for her help becoming so burdensome and thus been less forthcoming with her assistance, there would never have been an issue. She was so pleased to be recognized for her skills and abilities that she actually invited her impossible workload. She was blinded by her own popularity. By the time she realized that such demands on her time were almost impossible to meet, she had set a precedent. When she balked, others saw her as withholding and a whiner.

You Are Never Finished Getting Off to a Good Start

It is vital to remember that in any new situation you need to prove yourself. And even after you have established a stellar reputation, you cannot assume that you've got it made. There will always be people watching you and new people to deal with. Assume that you are as yet unproven with every new project, every new colleague, and every new customer.

Better to err on the side of caution and consistently strive to make large deposits in your corporate account, while taking only small withdrawals. The following chapters will reveal the secrets to making constant deposits to ensure that you become—and remain—a winner in your life at work.

Reality Check: How Are You Doing?

If you have taken a new job or joined a new team in the past 90 days, use the following questions as a measure of how effectively you are getting off to a good start and safeguarding against costly mistakes.

If you think you know the answer to a question, ask your self *how* you know. You want to be sure you are not operating on assumptions, but rather, on valid information from your own observations or those of a trusted source. If for any reason you are in doubt about an answer, double-check to confirm your perception.

This is by all means not a comprehensive list of everything you need to know, nor is every question relevant to your particular situation. However, the exercise is useful as a litmus test to indicate whether you are on the right track.

✦ Why was I selected for this position? How do the decision makers see me as adding value?

✦ Did I have a predecessor? Why did he or she leave? What were her or his strengths and weaknesses?

✦ Who are the stakeholders (boss, peers, direct reports)? Who are my internal and external customers? Can I answer the following about each of them?

   ✧ What is their role and responsibility?

   ✧ What do they need from me?

   ✧ What are their goals and priorities?

   ✧ What constitutes a "win" for them? How can I contribute to that?

✦ What do I know about my boss? How does he or she want me to communicate with him or her? How often? What about? What are his or her priorities?

+ Who on my team is considered to be successful? Why?

+ What are the sensitive issues and taboos? For my boss? For the team?

+ How does the team interact with one another—e-mail, phone, or face-to-face? How and when do they collaborate? When do they work independently?

+ Who should and should not be copied on e-mails, and under what circumstances?

+ What is the protocol for staff meetings and conference calls? How do I need to prepare for them?

+ Who are my primary sources of ongoing feedback? What have I learned from them?

PLAY NICE WITH EVERYONE

The Org Chart Isn't the Power Chart

Don't confuse title with power. The power structure in any organization is highly complex, ever-changing, and often difficult to fathom. Power is an extremely challenging subject to tackle, especially in 50,000 words or less. However, because power plays such a major role in the work world and is so important to how people fare, I can't ignore the topic. Understanding the power structure is essential to avoiding the mistakes that can undermine your career or steer it in the wrong direction.

On the surface, it would seem that power would solely be a function of title. The higher a person's name on the org chart, the more power he or she would have. If only it were that simple—how much easier our work lives would be! Unfortunately, identifying those with power is much more involved than finding out where their names are located on a chart.

Although a structured hierarchy and formal protocol are essential to accomplish anything and avoid total chaos, they are not the sole determinants of what really happens within any company. A number of factors and dynamics, in addition to title and standard procedures, determine the outcome of any issue, situation, or policy.

What Is Power?

The first step to understanding the dynamics of power is to be clear about what it is and how to recognize it.

The best way to define and determine the extent of an individual's power is by virtue of his or her capacity to influence the behavior of others in a meaningful way.

Power means influencing behavior. In other words, people take observable action in response to the direction or suggestion of a person with power. To sway the opinions or thinking of others does not constitute power unless this influence translates into some action.

> *John managed several telecommunications call centers and his staff frequently complained that the company's dress code was too strict, considering that they were never in front of the public. He brought the matter to the attention of the regional manager. Although he was able to convince her that the code was not necessary, he could not persuade her to change the requirements. Because John was unable to influence the regional manager to take action, he had no real power in this situation.*

Although organizational power includes the ability to influence the actions of others, there is more to it than that. These actions must be of consequence in that they either cause something to happen or prevent it from happening. The actions taken must have a visible and significant impact on the way business is conducted, internally or externally. Otherwise, from a practical perspective, the individual who influenced those actions had no real power in terms of how the company operates.

In the preceding example, if the regional manager had decided to revise the dress requirements because of John's input, it could be said that John was able to influence a change in the dress code. His power would have resulted from his ability to sway both the thinking and actions of the regional manager, with the outcome being a visible change in company policy.

The Sources of Power

Essentially, power comes either from having control of something that others want and consider valuable, or from the ability to influence those with that control. There are several sources of power within an organization:

+ Official

+ Incentive

+ Expertise/knowledge

+ Credibility

+ Access

One individual can have more than one source of power. Usually, the more sources he or she has, the greater his or her influence in any given situation.

Official Power

Official power is based on the understanding that people in a certain role, as defined by title, can request and expect certain behaviors of others by virtue of their control over valued resources: money, people, and time. They can grant, deny, or take away rewards such as raises, bonuses, promotions, and privileges. And of course, these people have the ability to hire and fire.

Although people with official power might have a vast span of authority and be the ultimate decision makers, their success is often contingent on the support, advice, and genuine cooperation and collaboration of others. In an organization of almost any size, the practice of autocratic management and unilateral decision making is a sure ticket to eventual failure, even if it results in a short-term change in the behavior of others.

A wise manager at any level knows that his or her success is ultimately dependent on others. He or she is also aware that others have data and expertise that she or he does not. Therefore, she or he looks to these people for information and counsel, and ultimately relies on others to champion and implement policies and decisions. Thus, there are other sources of power in addition to the official power that derives from a person's title.

> NOTE: *The power structure frequently varies from situation to situation according to who is involved and the source(s) of their power, what is at stake individually and collectively, and the significance of the outcome to the organization.*

Incentive Power

Incentive power comes from control over rewards or something else that other people want. I have stated that those with official power decide on the allocation of resources and incentives such as raises. However, people can have control over additional kinds of goodies.

A colleague or team of colleagues influences who is selected for important projects or task forces. Peers frequently seek partnerships on prized assignments that provide development opportunities and lead to future successes. Nominations for special awards or recognition often come from anywhere in the organization. Additionally, proactive backing and support can be a valuable commodity to someone who is advocating a particular project or course of action. Although people with control over these kinds of incentives cannot directly mandate how others act, they often have influence over those who are aware that they are in such a position.

> *Sally was a member of an expanding task force to centralize internal cost centers such as IT and accounting. Ken was interested in participating in this project and he was aware that Sally could endorse him. Knowing that, when he and Sally were collaborating on routine assignments, he would often seek her opinion and follow her*

lead. He wanted Sally to see him as a team player, willing to collaborate and cooperate. Although Sally could not mandate that Ken adapt to her way of doing things—and perhaps even had no interest in doing so—she nevertheless influenced Ken's behavior because she could help him attain something he valued.

Judy was the office manager supervising 10 administrative staff members. Alan, one of her direct reports, had been there many years and had a good deal of influence with the rest of the administrative people. They trusted him with their confidences and respected his viewpoints and opinions. He was in a position to rally them to enthusiasm or, conversely, influence them to take a negative view of an issue. Judy frequently sought his counsel and unless there was a good reason to the contrary, she followed his advice. Alan's ability to deliver the cooperation and support of the administrative people was incentive for Judy to comply with his requests and suggestions.

Expertise/Knowledge Power

Expertise/knowledge power belongs to those who have a critical skill or knowledge relevant to reaching a specific goal or bringing about a crucial outcome. In this situation, it is the recognition and value of the expertise or skill that influences others' decisions and actions.

Sam was a networking specialist called upon to advise senior management of an international money-transfer company on reconfiguring its Wide Area Network. In deference to Sam's expertise, management followed his suggestions on the purchase of all hardware and software without question. In addition, the decisions they made regarding network language, security, and the solutions to routine operations were in line with his recommendations. So even though Sam wasn't the one signing the checks, he held most of the power in that situation. Indeed, he was essentially the person who designed and configured the system, and ultimately determined how it would be managed.

Credibility Power

Credibility power derives from how well one is regarded by others. Is he or she trustworthy? Is he or she known to be reliable and competent? Do others confide in him or her and act on his or her advice? Credibility power is usually accrued over time, and it increases through word-of-mouth as a person's reputation spreads throughout the organization. If someone is seen as trustworthy and believable, he or she has the power to influence others, both above and below, based on credibility alone.

> *A credit card company was in need of new branding to reverse a significant loss of business over the past several years. It had a global team that worked with regional presidents worldwide. The prevailing practice was that each country used a different agency to develop a different strategy and campaign.*

> *Joanne was chief marketing officer and executive vice president of global marketing. Her competence was well documented. She had a reputation for being a team player, reliable and trustworthy, and not motivated by power considerations or self-promotional interests. Even though she did not have the authority to mandate it, Joanne was able to leverage her credibility to influence the adoption of one fundamental strategy implemented globally, with only minor tweaking as necessary to incorporate cultural differences.*

Access Power

Access power belongs to those who have the ear of those with the preceding sources of power. It can come about as a result of a formal reporting relationship, physical proximity, prior history, or mutual interests and goals.

Those with access power control the flow of information that gets to the power holders. They tell the leaders what is going on in the organization, and who is doing and saying what. Frequently they are asked to share their perspective on problems and solutions. They are usually also privy to information that others are not.

> *Arthur had been the executive assistant to Penny, the Senior Partner of a prestigious law firm, for many years. He became privy to in-fighting between two junior partners that was jeopardizing the case of a valued client and felt an obligation to apprise Penny of the sit-uation. As a result, the case was reassigned. Arthur had the power to influence this outcome because of his easy access to Penny.*

> NOTE: *Whether a person has power and from what it derives is subject to constant change. A major error in judgment can cause a person with credibility power to go from hero to goat almost overnight. Changes in technology or the marketplace can alter the knowl-edge and expertise that are considered valuable. Shifts in senior management can change who has access at that level.*

The Exercise of Power

Power is the ability to make things happen or prevent them from hap-pening—not just by mandate or veto, but by virtue of influencing oth-ers to take definitive actions that bring about a desired result. The following example illustrates how power actually plays out.

> *Ken, vice president of sales for the Midwestern region of an auto-parts manufacturing company, wanted to implement a more regi-mented approach and detailed documentation of sales activity. To that end, he introduced new software that required a vast amount of research and information about prospective and current customers, as well as entailing considerable time to develop a strategic plan and doc-ument relationship building, sales activity, and results.*

Ken personally presented the new system at each of the field offices with the mandated endorsement of the sales managers. It wasn't too long after they started using the software that the sales staff began to complain. They found the system to be onerous and felt that it was detracting from productive time that could be spent with customers developing relationships and generating sales.

Steve was a valued sales manager with one of the highest-producing territories. He had actually declined the regional VP position before it was offered to Ken. He knew that Ken's insistence on replicable structures had previously been considered a strength, but was seen as excessive and a detriment to his effectiveness in his current role.

Steve subtly suggested to his direct reports that for the time being they make "educated guesses" instead of diligently capturing and recording all the required data. As the other sales managers became aware of this practice, it quietly spread across all the field offices under Ken's purview. Eventually, these reports became more a matter of "cut and paste" than an accurate reflection of sales strategy and activity.

After several months, with the support of the other sales managers, Steve approached Ken about the system. In response to their concerns about a negative impact on sales, and suggestions for more time-effective methods for collecting streamlined data, Ken agreed to discontinue the use of the software.

Ken had the official power to authorize the purchase of the software, introduce the system to the field, and insist on the public support of the sales managers. However, in the long run, he was unable to effect a real change on the sales staff's practices. Steve could be said to have the ultimate power in that he was able to influence the field to circumvent the system, and to ultimately convince Ken to drop it. Even if Ken had insisted on the continued use of the software, the sales representatives were only going through the motions, so Ken would not have really influenced any meaningful change in their behavior.

Let's examine the sources of Steve's power. He had the official power to suggest that his direct reports minimize time and effort spent in data gathering and documentation. His credibility with the rest of the sales managers and their salespeople influenced them to adopt this same practice.

Steve was willing to risk undermining Ken in this manner because he was aware of his own earned credibility and he was armed with the information as to how his superiors perceived Ken's management style. Eventually, Steve's credibility with and access to Ken led to the discontinuance of the system. Thus Steve, by the judicious exercise of his power, was able to prevent something from occurring in the sales organization.

The outcome might have been quite different if Steve had not had the results and credibility he enjoyed, or if Ken's superiors regarded his management practices differently. Steve's power was not absolute, but rather was due to a particular set of circumstances. Under even slightly different conditions, the power structure and dynamics could have been very different.

> *CAUTION: Note that Steve did not flaunt his resistance, nor did he encourage others to do so. Conference call agendas did not include this item, and official or unofficial documentation regarding this stealth mutiny was nowhere to be found. And eventually Steve engaged Ken by acknowledging his official power and making the case to drop the system.*

Steve dealt with situation quietly. Had he openly challenged Ken's authority, requiring the public endorsement of Ken's superiors, the outcome would have been quite different. It can get extremely messy for an organization to openly condone the defiance of its official power structure.

Virtual Alert

In today's business environment, where there is never enough time, reliance on e-mail is second-nature and the most expedient means of communication. Exercise extreme caution to avoid releasing toxic evidence of insubordination or challenges to the official power structure into cyberspace.

The previous discussion does not mean that you must analyze down to the last detail who has what power, how much, and from where it derives. It does underscore, however, that power is not an absolute commodity. It arises from different sources, varies according to a number of circumstances, and is different from situation to situation.

Therefore, in order to avoid misinterpreting the power structure and letting it get in your way, approach each new situation or issue from two related yet different strategies:

+ Do not disregard or alienate either current or future power holders in the ordinary course of doing business.

+ Identify the power holders who are in a position to help you obtain a specific goal or objective.

In the first instance, you need to assume that you do not know who has or will have power. In the second, you need to figure it out.

Build Relationships Up, Down, and Across

Relationships are a key part of your professional success. The following sections detail the fundamentals of building effective work relationships.

Engage People Outside Your Department

In Secret 1 I talked about engaging the people that you deal with in the course of doing your job. As these relationships become solidified, it is time to expand beyond those to include people outside your immediate work environment.

You can come in contact with others through mutual relationships, company meetings, and social gatherings. Be alert to opportunities to volunteer for committees and take internal training courses or workshops. Strike up casual conversations in the break room. You can also call on others outside your work group for their expertise or advice about a particular problem or issue. People are flattered to be recognized in this way and will usually be eager to help.

Take every opportunity to get to know others. Express a genuine interest in them. Ask questions and listen carefully to the answers. Pay attention to the names of spouses, names and ages of children, hobbies, vacation plans, and preferences, and so on. Ask about their career history and goals, current projects, and professional strengths and challenges. Engage in conversations about your common interests, professional and personal.

Based on your interactions, demonstrate your attention and interest in others by being alert to little things you can do for them. For example:

+ Direct them to a relevant Web site.

+ Contact them after an important meeting to see how it went.

+ Send them a news article about something that interests them.

John got his Ph.D. in chemistry and joined a research and development division of a mineral-processing company. He selected this particular organization over others because they were known to allocate resources toward the development of cutting-edge technology and processes.

John worked hard and kept up with advances in his field. He quickly identified business priorities and customer needs, and his work reflected the requirements of both. He worked cooperatively with the others on his team and was careful to build a relationship with his boss.

He had been with the company a little over two years when he learned of a special project to develop a new processing technique. John informed his boss of his desire to be part of the team and was assured he would receive every consideration. However, he was overlooked for this assignment with the explanation that those chosen had more experience.

The reality, however, was that John was not known to anyone outside his own department. He had failed to cultivate relationships outside his direct work team. He was highly introverted and it took a great deal of energy to interact with others, especially in non–work-related, casual situations. Therefore, John neglected to reach out and engage peers and management outside his own work group. He was essentially unknown to most of the organization.

It was vital that the team members of this important project work together effectively and cooperatively with no in-fighting or one-upmanship. John did not have any champions other than his boss. Consequently, given how crucial the project was to the company, his boss's recommendation alone was not sufficient to convince the decision makers to include John, especially because they had a large number of others to choose from.

Earn Endorsements

Over time relationships can become a source of valuable information. They can also help you to get what you want. But before others will offer support, they need to have confidence in you. Do you produce quality work? Can you be trusted? Do you treat others appropriately? How do you handle stress and conflict situations? Do you meet deadlines and show consideration for your colleagues?

When another person endorses you, his or her reputation is at stake. If you in any way fall short, it is a reflection on them. He or she needs to be sure that you are competent, reliable, and trustworthy, and will make a valuable contribution to the project, department, and organization.

Never underestimate the power of anyone to back you—or worse, to get in your way. Because of the varied sources of power and the number of people who have access to decision makers, anyone and everyone can have a certain amount of power in any given situation. Because it is not always readily apparent or predictable, the safest course of action is to be diligent in building relationships and acknowledging everyone with whom you have contact.

> *CAUTION:* *How you are known and regarded by others plays a key role in your career progress. However, this does not mean that you can substitute skill and knowledge deficiencies for connections to people who can help move your career forward. You will want to take the initiative to ensure that you are competent and current in your field, in addition to engaging the support and endorsement of others.*

Respect Everyone Equally

It's essential to develop relationships based on genuine interest in and concern for others. Relationships should be reciprocal and valued for their own sake, not because of how they might work to your advantage someday.

True, you need the information, insight, and support that others provide. However, that is not what should drive your behavior in creating and maintaining professional relationships. Remember, differential treatment is noticed not only by those being treated as lesser, but also by those whose favor you are cultivating.

> *Barbara was a project manager for a computer manufacturing company. She had an eye to move to client services, which would expand her professional contacts both inside and outside the company. In order to build relationships outside her immediate work group, she was a frequent volunteer for community outreach and other projects the company sponsored.*
>
> *Barbara relied heavily on the administrative staff and frequently turned to them to help with her workload. She would often seek their*

assistance with her community activities and extracurricular projects. She was profuse in expressing her appreciation and frequently brought them little gifts to acknowledge their assistance.

Barbara was becoming increasingly well known outside her own department and she deliberately sought out and built relationships with people who had the power and influence to help her land a spot in client services. She was sure her efforts were about to pay off when a new position was created and she made it known that she wanted to be considered. She felt that she had good coaches and support, and was certain that she was a strong contender. However, when the decision was finally made, Barbara was surprised to learn that someone from the outside was hired to fill the position.

When she sought feedback, the official response was that the person hired had a stronger technical background. However, that was not the whole story. It was actually comments from some of the administrative staff that kept her from getting the job. They felt she treated them like second-class citizens in assuming she could pawn off work on them. They were only too aware of her differential treatment of them over others who had something to offer. Her efforts to show her appreciation were experienced as insincere and gratuitous, and served only to reinforce the perception that she was much too full of herself.

Not only were the administrative people offended, but others began to suspect her motives and came to see her as opportunistic and phony. They eventually came to feel that they were being used to advance Barbara's career.

"It's not what you know, it's who you know" has become a tired platitude that Barbara misinterpreted to mean that success is all about schmoozing with people who can do something for you. This connotation has led some to totally dismiss relationship building and view it as contrived, while others have translated it into disingenuous overtures that eventually come to be seen as phony and self-serving. Barbara made the mistake of focusing on people she thought could help her to the exclusion of others, thus raising doubts in everyone's mind as to her motives and sincerity.

Virtual Alert

If you work in an organization with multiple sites, be sure to build relationships virtually. Make sure your e-mails and your phone conversations are personable. When appropriate, elect to communicate by phone rather than e-mail.

Especially in e-mails, it's easy to be all business and sometimes even curt. Don't forget a salutation, and it helps to say something casual like "I hope you are not too overwhelmed by the computer conversion," or "I understand you're having an unusual amount of tornado activity this year." When you are requesting a response from someone, acknowledge how busy he or she is and ask for the information ASAP only when necessary.

On the phone, inquire about the individual while being cautious not to get too personal. Questions about how work is going, if they enjoyed a weekend or holiday, and the like are ways to establish a more amiable relationship than by sticking strictly to business. Do be careful, however, not to engage in this practice to the extent that people feel that you are wasting their time and keeping them from their work.

Action Items

❏ Stay current on your company's intranet or newsletter and note opportunities to contribute to and participate with others.

❏ Identify opportunities to develop relationships outside your department.

❏ Make a list of people outside your immediate workgroup whom you might contact for information or advice.

(CONTINUED)

(CONTINUED)

> ❐ Pay close attention to personal and professional information about those with whom you come in contact.
>
> ❐ As your circle of relationships grows, it might be helpful to record this information to prompt your memory when you anticipate coming in contact with someone.

Hitch Your Wagon to More than One Star

People with power can be here today and gone tomorrow. Anyone can come and go in an instant for any number of reasons. A loss of power or shift in the power structure can be sudden, or it can happen slowly—almost imperceptibly—over a period of time. Sometimes it's predictable; other times it's a surprise. Therefore, it's important not to count on any one person's coattails as your ticket to stardom.

Putting this advice into practice might not be as easy as it seems. When meetings, "to dos," e-mails, and constant fires are popping up in your face and lurking over your shoulder, it is easy to rely on your existing relationships and contacts as though they will be there forever. However, you want to make it a constant practice to continue to build relationships whenever the opportunity presents itself, and to deliberately create situations to develop new relationships as your time and schedule allow.

> *Leslie was involved in a special project to identify third-party distributors and cost-effective shipping partners for a food products manufacturing company. Kathleen, the director of logistics, was the internal customer. Leslie soon caught Kathleen's attention by demonstrating her competence, savvy, and hard work. Over time, even though Leslie was several levels below Kathleen, their relationship developed into a friendship as they discovered they had much in common.*

Kathleen was a major player and well respected throughout the organization. She had earned the confidence, and was a protégée of the COO, to whom she directly reported. Although Leslie's friendship was not motivated by Kathleen's position in the company, she could not help but be aware of Kathleen's potential to influence and advance her career.

When the COO was recruited away by his former mentor, the president of a competitor, he convinced Kathleen to go with him. Although Leslie remained in contact with Kathleen, she had lost a major source of support and endorsement inside the company.

Kathleen was hesitant to follow the COO because she had established her reputation independent of her association with him. However, she felt a certain amount of loyalty and was convinced that his continued support could only serve to further her career options.

Unfortunately, after the first 18 months at the new company, the president came into disfavor and was asked to step down. Soon after, both the COO and Kathleen were replaced.

Ignore These Thoughts!

If you find these thoughts running through your mind, don't listen to them!

- ✦ "I know a lot of important people will be at the reception, but I've just got too much work to take the time to go."
- ✦ "Now that Judy is my mentor and champion, I've got it made in this company."
- ✦ "I'm just too tired to socialize with these people after sitting in meetings with them all day."

Don't Underestimate Your Own Power

It is not unusual to overlook your own power, especially when it derives from a source other than title or ultimate decision-making authority. If you fail to take the sources of your influence into account, you are at risk of being seen as using power inappropriately or in a devious manner.

Be aware of how others might see you in terms of your credibility, expertise, information, and access to decision makers. Once you have identified your power in any specific situation, be sure to exercise it above board and with integrity. If you choose to abuse your power and people come to distrust you as a result, it is next to impossible to regain that trust.

> *Joshua, manager of event and meeting planning for an international hotel chain, had a close connection with Edith, the president. Their relationship began when they started with the company as peers and spanned many years. They had become personal friends as well as professional colleagues and everyone in the organization was aware of their affiliation.*
>
> *Joshua and Edith often turned to one another for counsel and each found it useful to bounce ideas off the other. When Joshua saw things differently than his colleagues, he counted on Edith to help him think through the situation and advise him as to how to handle it.*
>
> *On occasion, if the issue was critical and Joshua did not have enough influence over a situation to steer it in the direction they both thought it should go, Edith felt the need to intervene. She would do so only when absolutely necessary, and she was careful not to refer to her discussions with Joshua.*
>
> *When Edith moved on, Joshua was surprised to discover the extent to which he had alienated others because of his relationship with her. They had come to distrust him and, with Edith out of the picture, he was unable to gain the cooperation or confidence of his coworkers.*

Joshua was not motivated by power, but by genuine interest in doing the right thing. To that end, he turned to Edith as a confidante after many years of friendship. In spite of the best intentions of both, when Edith would get involved, others experienced her intervention as Joshua's power play. They were certain that Joshua deliberately went to Edith to use that relationship to manipulate the situation in his favor. Over time, they began to back down in conflict situations. Joshua interpreted their acquiescence as agreement with his point of view.

Power is often in the eyes of the beholder, and Joshua failed to take into account how his relationship with Edith was perceived by others. Had he been more attuned to his own power, he could have handled certain situations in another manner.

Joshua needed to be clear with Edith upfront about which conversations could remain between the two of them, and under which circumstances Edith would feel duty-bound to intervene. In the latter case, Joshua needed to involve others in the situation before approaching Edith. He could explain that Edith had strong opinions on the issues and would want to be apprised. Then Joshua and his colleague(s) could together bring the matter to Edith's attention. This would let others know that their input was considered valuable and allow them to better understand Edith's thinking. It would also serve to let others see that Edith did not always agree with Joshua, thus avoiding the perception that Joshua resorted to end-runs in order to get his way.

Virtual Alert

If you are physically located near power holders and have peers that are geographically distant, this close proximity is a source of power in that you have access that others do not. Just by virtue of the circumstances, you are at risk of being perceived as taking advantage of the situation. You will need to be extra cautious to refrain from any words or actions that could give credence to that perception.

(CONTINUED)

(CONTINUED)

Don't make constant referrals to conversations and collaborations with that person. Resist the temptation to speak for her or him, such as "I know that Tom would say…" or "Jane asked me to tell you that…."

In addressing differences of opinion, do not flaunt your access and one-up a peer by conferring with the power holder without including your colleague in the conversation. An e-mail or phone conversation that includes the sentence "I checked with Gary and he absolutely agrees with me about that," will foster resentment that can come back to bite you when you least expect it.

Avoid volunteering information that flaunts your close proximity to the boss, such as "John sometimes is preoccupied when he's talking on the phone and doesn't really listen well. If you want him to back that project, send a detailed e-mail and ask for a time to talk about it," or "I told Emma that you had some really good ideas about the product launch and she's looking forward to hearing from you." You might mean well, but it could sound like you're gloating.

If you are a manager where one or more of your direct reports is down the hall and others are not, be careful not to put those in your location in awkward positions that might be interpreted by their peers as your "playing favorites" or them taking advantage of the situation. Don't ask them to relay messages for you and be careful to distribute the plum assignments equally. Make an extra effort to include those at a distance and talk things over with them just as you do with the individual(s) who are just a few steps away.

Action Items

☐ List projects, task forces, and any special teams you are on and identify what kind of power, if any, you might have.

☐ Take stock of people to whom you have access and assess whether others might perceive you to be in a position of power.

Don't Overestimate Your Power

Sometimes it's easy to get caught up in your title and assume that people will do what you ask merely because of your position. The following is a cautionary example.

Tim, a human resource manager, was charged with creating a structured process for the professional development of bank employees across multiple locations. He introduced a highly complex system requiring ambitious goals that managers and their direct reports were expected to discuss and document. The managers complied by filling out the plan, but many did not enforce or support adherence to it because they felt it was unrealistic and costly in terms of both time and money.

Eventually, the exercise was seen as a meaningless gesture of no real consequence. Because he was receiving the completed professional development forms documenting that the required discussions were being held, Tim was not aware that the process was not being implemented as it was intended.

During a period of intense competition for talent, the company was losing a number of valued employees to other banking institutions.

(CONTINUED)

(CONTINUED)

During exit interviews, one of the most frequently stated reasons for leaving was the lack of professional development opportunities. When this came to the attention of the VP of human resources, Tim was fired for failing to deliver on an important project.

Tim's predicament was borne of two faulty assumptions. The first was that his title and role in human resources would be sufficient to influence the adoption and implementation of the professional development system. The second was that the documentation was an accurate representation of what was really happening.

When you have a responsibility to deliver in a situation where you are dependent on the cooperation of others, especially when you cannot directly observe the conduct of those who have to comply, take steps to earn their support and get their input. Relying solely on your position on the org chart won't necessarily get the job done.

In Tim's case, he would have been better served by engaging others in the planning stages of the employee-development initiative. Input from the managers who had to live with it would have enabled him to adapt it to their needs and therefore, eliminated resistance. Furthermore, their early participation would have earned their investment in the success of the program. After introducing the plan, he needed to get feedback to understand how it was working and what modifications, if any, were necessary to make it more user-friendly and effective.

Ignore These Thoughts!

If you find these thoughts running through your mind, don't listen to them!

+ "I know the IT people think the documentation is onerous, but they will have to do it anyway."

+ "I've got to get this done fast. I don't have time to be talking to every Tom, Dick, and Sally about it."

+ "The more people involved, the more complicated it gets and it takes too long to get anything done."

In some instances, the process of how you introduce a change is as important as the actual quality of what it is. Even if you can get people to go through the motions, you are not successful unless something meaningful happens as a result of your efforts. It can be risky to assume that by virtue of your position, even with the backing of those with official power and authority, you will have the influence necessary to accomplish your mission.

Action Items

In the early planning stage of a project or initiative be sure to do the following:

☐ Identify those in the organization who will be impacted, how they will be affected, and what will be required of them.

☐ Ask for input and participation from people who have credibility with and influence over the affected parties.

☐ If appropriate, engage the affected parties in a task force or other process to develop and introduce the new program, and incorporate their feedback as often as possible.

☐ Monitor progress after implementation and make necessary changes and modifications.

Stay Out of "Partisan Politics"

Numerous issues arise within an organization where people do not see eye-to-eye. These can range from differing ideas on the right customer solution, to how to best solve a problem, to the future direction of the business. Or they might just be the result of personality conflicts and differences. As such situations continue, they can turn into hot buttons about which people become sharply divided. The whole matter takes on a meaning far deeper than the issue itself and becomes quite personal to those involved in the debate.

When feathers get ruffled, even though people might not remember all the details, they never forget who was with them or against them. The potential harm of taking sides far outweighs any possible benefits, no matter what the ultimate outcome is. By taking a public stand, you are certain to antagonize someone.

Even if at the moment, those in favor are more powerful within the company than those opposed, circumstances can shift. Those who can influence your fate a year or two down the road might be those against whom you previously took a stand. And they *will* remember.

The safest approach in highly charged situations is to, if at all possible, stay out of them. Do not get involved or make any comments to anyone about your opinion. Those who remain above the fray usually fly under the radar of those who are entrenched. Even if you think the whole thing is silly and out of control, *keep it to yourself!* Anything you say is in jeopardy of being repeated, and more likely, distorted.

Ignore These Thoughts!

If you find these thoughts running through your mind, don't listen to them!

+ "I think this whole debate is unnecessary and I'm going to say so at the meeting."

+ "I know exactly what we should do and it's time we do it and move on."

+ "Certainly Tina will keep it confidential if I tell her what I really think about all this."

If you are in a situation in which you must take a public stand, do not get yourself firmly dug in. Look at the problem objectively—apart from the emotions of the issue—and find the merits and disadvantages of each viewpoint. Put yourself in the role of a facilitator toward a solution, rather than a proponent of one side or the other. Listen closely to all sides and encourage them to consider the others' point of view.

CAUTION: *In attempting to work toward a solution without taking one particular position, be careful that you do not appear wishy-washy. Staying out of conflict situations does not mean that you go whichever way the wind is blowing at the moment. You do not want to seem to agree with one perspective one day only to turn around to endorse the advantages of a totally opposite point of view the next.*

Plan Ahead and Anticipate Opportunities

You have been careful not ignore anyone or step on any toes. You are now focusing on how you want your career to progress and in what direction. To realize your goals, you will want to take advantage of opportunities such as new positions being created, a promotion anticipated in your or another department, special projects, new business initiatives in the offing, or other such happenings that represent career growth opportunities.

An important part of your strategy will be to identify and engage those people who have the power to help you reach your goals. This is fairly clear-cut when you are seeking such things as a raise, an educational experience, or another opportunity where your boss is most likely the key influencer and decision maker. However, in many other circumstances, several people have the power to affect the outcome. Even though there might be one ultimate decision maker, others will influence that decision.

If you want to be considered for such opportunities, you need to be able to identify and talk to those people with the power to support you.

A good deal of advance planning and activity often precedes the formal announcement of any new opportunities. Usually at the time the information is made public and available to all, decisions have already been made or they are well on their way to being finalized. Those who want to participate in and benefit from new challenges must get involved early in the process. This requires that you anticipate what is coming down the road, when, and who will be involved.

It is by way of the relationships you have developed that you can learn of potential opportunities in sufficient time to pursue them. Everyone in the company is in a position to know about what is happening behind the scenes, what kind of plans are in the offing, and who is involved.

The best way to ensure advance notice about opportunities that might interest you is to make sure contacts know what you are looking for. This means you need to do some upfront planning around your goals. The people who you want to support you need to know what you want in order to route the appropriate information to you.

Action Items

❐ Identify one or two short-term career goals.

❐ If you don't already have the information, contact the appropriate people to learn what you need to do to reach those goals.

❐ Talk to your manager about education or work assignments that will help you achieve your goals.

❐ Be sure to tell your contacts what you are seeking and ask whether they have any advice or suggestions of others you might talk to.

Know What Power Holders Want

Once you have identified the people who will be making recommendations and decisions, you have to understand their role and what they have at stake before you approach them. You want to show them how you have the ability to make them successful, and then speak from the perspective of what you have to offer, not what you want to gain for yourself.

You might be able to get this information from the same people who tell you about the opportunity or from others who are in the loop. Under some circumstances it is appropriate to ask the stakeholders themselves. When there are several stakeholders, you cannot assume that what is important to one is the same for another. One person might be seeking cutting-edge technical experience; another is concerned with ease of application; and yet a third is interested in cost-effectiveness.

Sally, an up-and-coming corporate lawyer for a large chain of retail stores, learned of a team being put together to work on a high-profile discrimination lawsuit, most likely bogus, but potentially costly to defend against. She was well versed in employment law, and had successfully settled similar cases for her previous company. Her reputation in the legal community was that she was tough but reasonable.

Sally learned that Frank was head legal counsel and would be selecting the team members. She did not know Frank personally but had several relationships with people who did. She asked them to tell him of her interest and past experience, and emphasize her superior negotiation skills and track record for getting the lowest possible settlements. After they had talked to Frank about her, Sally sent him a follow-up e-mail to request they talk personally.

Frank thanked her for her interest but replied that he had already identified the people he needed. Sally was unable to get any feedback to explain why she wasn't given the opportunity to at least be considered for the team. She concluded it was due to cronyism and soon opted to leave the company to seek an organization that would provide her with better opportunities.

Sally's mistake was assuming that the organization wanted to settle the case. In fact, due to the importance of public opinion, the senior team had decided to make public relations a priority. They wanted this case to be dropped entirely or go to court. Consequently, they were looking for top-notch trial attorneys who would be able to clear the company's reputation, which was brought into question merely by the filing of the suit.

One Last Reminder: Never Fail to Follow Protocol

Just because events in the organization don't always occur by the book, according to title and formal protocol, does not mean that either can be ignored. You must always adhere to policy even though you know that what's happening behind the scenes is what will determine the actual outcome of any situation.

It is *always* a mistake to disregard the formal power structure. Be sure to copy the appropriate people on e-mails, follow the prescribed procedures for applying for a different job, and include those who should be involved in any specific situation. Be absolutely certain that you never do anything publicly to indicate that you know that someone who supposedly has the power might not really be the strongest or only influencer.

Reality Check: How Are You Doing?

The following questions can serve as a guide to preventing costly errors due to misinterpreting or misunderstanding the power structure in your organization. You can also use it to assess how to approach specific situations and identify how to reach important goals.

This is by all means not a comprehensive list of everything you need to know, nor is it implied that every question is relevant to your particular situation. However, the exercise is useful as a litmus test to indicate whether you are on the right track.

✦ What is the formal power structure in my workgroup?

✦ Who else has power and influence in my workgroup? What kind of power?

✦ What other groups and departments do I work with or have contact with? What is the formal and informal power structure in those groups?

+ What power and influence do I have over others inside and outside my workgroup? From where does it derive? How do I know?

+ Who is looking to me for support because of my power? What do they want? Am I willing to support them?

+ What can I do to increase my incentive, expertise/knowledge, credibility, or access power?

+ What are the opportunities for me to increase my internal network? What are the upcoming social gatherings? Are there committees or volunteer activities that I can participate in?

+ What do I need to do to maintain and enhance my current relationships?

+ What are the controversial issues in my department? In the company? Which, if any, do I need to get involved with? How can I handle it without alienating one side or the other?

+ What are my short-term career or work goals? Who has the power to support me in achieving them? What are those people looking for?

YIELD THE FLOOR

Being Right Doesn't Always Mean Being Smart

Although we are conditioned throughout our lives to find the "right" answer, do the "right" thing, and avoid doing "wrong," when crossing the corporate threshold, that kind of black-and-white thinking can lead to trouble. It is best to do away with those polar perspectives and eliminate from your vocabulary the words that represent them. The notions of "right and wrong" can be replaced with "practical," "realistic," "cost-effective," "doable," "low risk," and other such criteria for action. This perspective allows for much more flexibility in response to the complex dynamics that dictate what actually goes on in the workplace.

When there are differences about how to solve a problem, achieve a goal, or explain successes or failures, it can be counterproductive to tackle the issue from the standpoint that there is only one right answer or approach. And even if you believe that is the case, and even when you are certain you have the "right" answer, it can be a serious mistake to campaign relentlessly for one point of view.

Don't take this to mean that you refrain from offering your ideas or back down at the first sign of any disagreement. It is your responsibility to focus on creating the best possible outcome for the company. The optimum strategy is to balance what is good for the company with a sensitivity to the stakes and needs of others. It serves no useful purpose to persist beyond a point that is constructive, and in the process, risk alienating others.

Stacy was attending a senior management meeting of a computer networking corporation about to initiate a significant shift in its product and service offerings. After the CEO enthusiastically presented the details of the changes and what they meant to the future of the company, Stacy pointed out the lack of internal systems and processes to support the transition. She expressed concern that the expected results would not be realized without them.

The CEO thanked Stacy for her observation and was about to move on. But Stacy would not let the issue drop. She was passionate in her conviction that the initiatives would collapse without the proper infrastructure to sustain them. When the CEO pushed back, she was sure that it must be because she had not communicated effectively. Stacy was so certain she was right that she could not imagine that anyone would disagree if she could just find the right words to present her case.

She did not notice the fidgeting of her colleagues as she relentlessly pursued the matter with the CEO. Stacy was the only one oblivious to the mounting tension in the room until she was at last asked, quite sternly, to please sit down. Humiliated, she spent the next several hours sulking in her hotel room, wondering whether she would ever live down that sorry episode.

Unfortunately, she did not. The story became company lore and her poor judgment at that meeting seemed to taint her every contribution and achievement thereafter.

Stacy had been motivated only by her desire to see the successful introduction of new products and services, and by her firm belief that she knew what was necessary for that to happen. She was so intent on what she believed to be the right course of action that she failed to consider how she was publicly putting the CEO on the spot and bringing his competence into question. In addition, she was unaware that she was asking him to do something that was not in his power to accomplish. He was under extreme pressure from the board of directors to increase shareholder value and the announcement of the new offerings was meant to do just that. He did not have the luxury of taking the time it would require to develop and implement the internal processes that Stacy was so zealously insisting upon. Nor could he publicly state that he was motivated by the need to make something dramatic happen on Wall Street.

Theoretically, Stacy had assessed the situation correctly and it could be said that she was "right" to assert the need for an infrastructure to support the new products and services. However, in the work world, the word "right" can be overused, and sometimes overrated. There are frequently many factors to consider when choosing a course of action. Often there is more than one path to a successful outcome.

Expect—and Respect—Personal Agendas

In an uncomplicated world, everyone would agree on what was best for the company and only those considerations would come into play. No one would operate from his or her own personal and professional interests, and differences of opinion would revolve solely around what would produce the mutually agreed-upon desired outcome. Guess what—this doesn't happen nearly as often as you might think!

Agendas Based on Job Responsibilities

Often, the mandates and responsibilities of different jobs lead to opposing interests and viewpoints. A purchasing agent is looking to control costs while an engineer is proposing the most technically advanced, and most expensive, solution. A salesperson wants to get the lowest pricing for a valued customer and the vice president of sales is aiming for the highest possible margins. An executive assistant, wanting to ensure his boss a nonstressful business trip with meetings that accommodate a demanding schedule, comes up against the company's travel agent, who has been told to keep travel costs to a minimum.

People are assessed and rewarded according to their ability to stay within the defined parameters and requirements of their jobs. These are usually defined in terms of metrics and set objectives. They are documented in performance reviews and often constitute the rationale for raises and promotions.

Agendas Based on Personal Needs and Objectives

There are also many other agendas that go beyond specific job requirements. These are the personal needs and professional objectives that are just as essential to job satisfaction, successful career management, and advancement in the workplace. Things such as gaining expertise on cutting-edge technology, visibility to senior management, and winning an important account do a great deal to further career success. The desire for these coups, and others like them, frequently explains how people arrive at one point of view over another.

All kinds of agendas influence people's perspectives and drive their actions. Everyone meets their needs and realizes their goals through their performance and work achievements. Every situation, problem, project, or assignment represents an opportunity to solidify a career, move closer to a goal, or achieve personal satisfaction. It only makes good sense to be alert to the personal and professional wins that can be achieved in the course of doing the job.

Serving personal needs is not only a fact—but often a requirement—of corporate life. The types of personal and professional stakes are as varied as the individuals who hold them. They may be directly related to work goals or reflect personal or lifestyle needs and desires. Following are just some of the possible agendas that can motivate behavior and attitudes:

+ To gain or remain in power

+ To achieve visibility

+ To stay on the cutting edge of technology

+ To get a raise

+ To be perceived as a problem solver

+ To make a case for telecommuting

+ To be seen as a leader

+ To gain recognition

+ To ensure consistency

+ To make a memorable contribution

+ To increase efficiency

+ To gain a new skill

+ To prove competence

+ To please a superior

+ To avoid risk

+ To overcome a reputation for indecisiveness

+ To beat out the competition

+ To be perceived as having superior technical expertise

+ To gain access to senior management

+ To be creative

+ To increase profitability

+ To be needed

+ To be seen as innovative

+ To gain credibility and influence

+ To be perceived as a risk taker

+ To be seen as a team player

+ To be in control

+ To reduce costs

+ To balance work and family needs

The list goes on and on. Innumerable personal and professional wins go undeclared and are not necessarily relevant to the stated company objective. And this in itself does not necessarily constitute a problem. People can be committed to both a quality result and meeting their own needs in the process of achieving it. Indeed, the two need not be mutually exclusive.

Discovering and Working with Other Agendas

As long as there is consensus among the involved parties, these personal and professional goals do not necessarily come into play, nor are they of any consequence in achieving the desired result. However, when differences arise, one or more of the parties just might be protecting what they have at stake personally or professionally. These goals become quite important to the person striving to reach them. Failure to take this into consideration can lead you to unknowingly step all over someone by focusing only on what you think is the best or the "right" answer.

When you are not in agreement with a colleague, consider whether he or she is motivated by an agenda and take this into account when you are determining how to proceed. You are wise to exercise caution in your choice of words and in how fervently you argue against another's point of view.

> *CAUTION: This does not mean that personal agendas should take precedence over all else. To honor them over what serves the company or contributes to the success and satisfaction of others is a potentially fatal mistake. To disregard everything in order to support an agenda for someone else or for yourself can be just as lethal as ignoring personal stakes. Each set of circumstances is different and requires a thoughtful approach and good judgment.*

Expect—and Respect—Hidden Agendas

Even though the term "hidden agendas" has a negative connotation, they run rampant in the workplace. I have already discussed the role personal agendas play in career success and satisfaction. Although some agendas are obvious due to a person's job responsibilities, others are not so apparent. And frequently you have to operate without a clue about what is motivating someone.

However, in some situations you might be able to discover another's agenda. It is appropriate to try to do so, if you proceed with suitable tact and respect. There is no exact script to find out about another's agenda; however, the process can, and should, be open and above board.

Verify What You Might Already Know

If you have had past dealings with the people involved, you might have some ideas about what they have to gain in a particular situation. Previous interactions and conversations might have provided insight about people's stakes, what is important to them, and what their goals are. Be alert to opportunities to have such exchanges before any issues arise. It is best to learn these things in advance of any controversy when the information is shared under neutral circumstances, with no judgments, energy around differences, or investment in outcomes.

Even though you might be able to make an educated guess about what someone has at stake, it is always a good idea to validate your perception. You might say something like "are you hoping that this project will provide you with a chance to work more closely with Henry?" or "The last time we talked you wanted to show your depth in this software. Are you hoping this will be your opportunity to do so?" Make sure that you approach the subject in a nonjudgmental and noncombative manner, and even better, as a way of learning how to help the other person achieve his or her personal or professional "win."

Ask People Directly

The best time to ask people about their personal stakes is before any disagreements or differences occur. At the beginning of a project or collaborative assignment, it is perfectly appropriate to discuss with those involved how the work or the outcome can serve to advance their personal or professional aspirations. In fact, this is the best time to do so.

Set the stage by acknowledging the wisdom and necessity for career management and how this might be an opportunity to not only do something good for the company, but also to help each other as well. You can do this individually or as a group. In fact, it is an excellent beginning to building a team. Again, the discussions take place in the absence of strong feelings about any particular issues. Initiate these early conversations, not just to avoid stepping on someone's professional toes, but because you are genuinely interested in supporting others in getting what they want. And don't forget: This is also an opportunity to engage their support for you.

Treat all conversations with coworkers about their personal and professional aspirations in general, or their specific stakes in a given situation, with the utmost appreciation and respect. Regard their disclosures as confidential, not discussed in their absence, and never used later in a manipulative manner in order to get your way or prove a point.

In some situations, it is inappropriate to initiate such conversations. You want to make sure that the relationship is solid enough and that the trust level is sufficient to justify asking such questions. Also, be certain that the culture condones that level of open disclosure. You want to be perceived as being interested and supportive of your colleagues, not as prying and inappropriate.

Seek Insight and Advice from Others

Sometimes, for some reason, asking the individual directly is not an option. In some circumstances, the relationship simply does not permit that kind of questioning. Or you might find yourself in an unexpected debate that has escalated to such a pitch that such an inquiry would only exacerbate the situation.

If you are participating in a heated conversation that feels more like a verbal tug-of-war than a professional discourse, if possible, suggest that the parties revisit the matter later. If you are in a meeting, it's a good time for a break. If the setting is less structured, you can cite a prior commitment with the promise to get back to the person or people involved at another time. As well as providing everyone with the opportunity to cool down, it also affords you time to do some intelligence gathering.

Either at the beginning of a new project or in the midst of a disagreement, you can speak to those with whom you have developed relationships to see whether they can offer some insight. In doing so, approach them in a manner that does not put them in an awkward situation. You don't want to sound as if you are asking someone to betray a confidence or take sides in a controversy.

Be positive and do not offer editorial comments about the person you are inquiring about. Also, be careful to phrase your request in a manner that does not seem like you are probing for confidential information. You might say such things as this:

> *Charlie and I see the priorities for the conversion quite differently. Could you offer any insight or ideas that might help me better understand his perspective?*

Or you might want to ask for more general information:

> *I will be working with Charlie on the conversion. Since we have never worked together before, I wonder if you have any suggestions on how I might support him and make us both successful.*

If you are successful in gaining some insight, if the relationship permits, confirm your assumptions with the other person or people involved. Broach the subject carefully and back away if she or he is hesitant to discuss it with you. Whether or not you are on target, if she or he is hesitant to disclose that kind of information, there is nothing constructive to be gained from pursuing the subject. There is no magic formula to prompt another to reveal their personal agenda. Sometimes you might be successful with your questioning; other times you will be left without a clue.

Negotiate from Personal Agendas

When you are able to openly discuss the other person's agenda, you can bring that into any discussion about differences of opinion on how to proceed. You can explore alternative ways that the person might meet his or her personal needs, or you can acquiesce in deference to what he or she has to gain. In either case, give the other person's agenda every consideration in arriving at any solution or course of action.

Even if there has not been an open discussion of personal agendas, if you have a good idea what someone's is, you can suggest alternatives that will meet those needs. You do not have to disclose what you are attempting to do, but by taking into consideration what the other person might have at stake, you might be able to reach an agreement that is satisfactory to all.

Action Items

❐ Identify a situation or project you are currently working on or will be in the future.

❐ List the others who are or will be involved.

❐ For each, identify what his or her personal agenda might be.

❐ If you think you know, make it a point to validate your assumption.

  ✦ If you do not know, set aside a time to ask him or her if appropriate.

  ✦ If not appropriate, identify and approach others who might be able to offer some insight.

  ✦ Be sure to record this information and refer to it, either to help others gain their wins or to consider what the wins are in cases of differing opinions.

Understand the Many Faces of Hidden Agendas

It is certainly more straightforward to deal with vested interests when people are aware of how they are influenced by their own needs, and willing to share that information publicly. Frequently, neither is the case. Although there are times when it is possible to bring hidden agendas out into the open, there are also many circumstances that don't lend themselves to that kind of disclosure.

Trust could be an issue. A person might not have had sufficient dealings with the others to determine whether to trust them. Or he or she might feel, rightly or wrongly, that there is reason *not* to trust others. In either case, a hidden agenda will remain so.

Another factor that determines whether people will reveal their agendas is the perceived acceptability or "political correctness" of their personal gain. The desire to learn a new skill or be appointed to a project team seems easier and safer to share than fear of losing a job or striving to gain the favor of upper management. Even though the latter agendas are not "bad" and need not interfere with a desirable outcome for the company, they are rarely revealed to others.

Sometimes these agendas even become obscured to the person who holds them, whether or not the agenda is felt to be politically acceptable. It is not at all unusual for an individual to be only marginally aware, or even totally unaware, of what is motivating his or her behavior. In the process of finding ways to defend their predispositions, people can become convinced that their opinion is well reasoned and in no way reflects their own needs or wishes.

Hidden Agendas Masquerading as Fact

To meet personal and professional needs, people often strive to build a strong case in "fact" for the direction they want to take. Once they have a mental picture or map of where they want to go, they construct their route with the information that will get them there. People gravitate toward the data that supports their preconceived notions and disregard or discredit information that does not. The more invested they are in their perception, the more this holds true.

This explains why arguments that counter another's point of view often fall on deaf ears. The more public and relentless the challenge, the more entrenched the individual becomes—and perhaps, the more annoyed. Eventually, it is possible that he or she comes to take the dispute personally and maintain a grudge toward the person who perpetuated it.

> *Tyler, the training manager of a retail clothing chain, was asked to select and collaborate with an external organization to design a training program for new store managers. He aspired to eventually join an instructional design company and had his eye on a firm in Canada, known in the business to be one of the best. Tyler saw this as an opportunity to develop relationships in that firm by engaging them to design the new manager training.*

> *Even though Tyler realized it was to his advantage to hire the Canadian company, that was not what he told himself as he went about accomplishing his business mission. Although Tyler's plan represented a sound career management strategy, he was not able to say to himself or anyone else "I'm going to hire these people no matter what because it is in my own best interest!"*

> *So he began with the premise that the Canadian company was the best organization to do the job and proceeded to find reasons why that was indeed the case. He checked its Web site, interviewed the principals, and got samples of their work. In checking references, Tyler talked to a former client who found them "inflexible" at times, but in exploring this further, Tyler concluded that the client lacked the sophistication to appreciate the expertise of the people at the Canadian company.*

When he researched other companies, it was not surprising that they did not measure up. There was always a good reason to eliminate them: They did not have sufficient experience in designing manager training; they took a cookie-cutter approach; their quality standards were not high enough.

By the time he was finished with his intelligence gathering, all signs were pointing Tyler in the direction he wanted to go. He was convinced that the Canadian company was the best choice for the job. And should anyone question his preference, he was armed with a litany of facts to support his selection.

As obvious as it might be to an observer that Tyler was constantly influenced by his preference to hire the Canadian company, he was not necessarily aware of how strongly his predisposition dictated his process and conclusions. And Tyler's experience is not at all unusual.

Hidden Agendas Posing as Opportunity

Another way people introduce and promote a personal agenda is to position it as an opportunity for the company. And as is the case when hidden agendas are presented as fact, by the time the idea's champion takes the case public, he or she is convinced that they are acting only in the best interest of the company. Pity the poor soul who might innocently poke holes in his or her argument by introducing information or ideas that contradict his or her conclusions.

Rebecca, a senior executive of a high-end furniture manufacturing company, was vying to be the first woman CEO in the history of her company. She felt that in order to be competitive, she needed to do something "big" to establish her ability to lead the organization.

She had just completed a symposium about a comprehensive strategy to make manufacturing enterprises more globally competitive. Rebecca

(CONTINUED)

(CONTINUED)

felt that introducing this methodology, if successful, would provide her with the visibility and credentials she needed to be a viable contender for the CEO position.

The first step was to sell this idea to the executive leadership team, so she went about gathering data to substantiate that this was an unprecedented opportunity to jump light years ahead of the competition. Just as Tyler did, she set about on her fact-finding mission with a bias toward data that supported the implementation of this new methodology and disregarded or explained away any information that did not. After gaining the approval of the senior team, she carefully selected the metrics that were most likely to validate the success of the new manufacturing strategy.

Hidden Agendas Camouflaged as Crises

Just as a personal agenda can be dressed up as an opportunity, so can it also be defined in terms of a problem or a crisis. A decline in revenues can be used to justify the introduction of a new product or sales strategy. A quality concern can be exploited to implement a new processing technology. Customer complaints provide the rationale for the launch of a relationship management initiative.

Once again, the data-gathering process will be dictated by an individual's desire to move in a particular direction. And once again, be cautious before taking a firm stand against the resulting recommendations.

Hidden Agendas Surfacing as Feedback

When seeking feedback from others to support an agenda, it's relatively easy to skew the information garnered by carefully phrasing the questions and interviewing those people most likely to offer the desired response. And, on those occasions when they do not provide answers that justify a particular direction or initiative, as with the other agenda disguises, there are ways to disregard or discredit them.

Taylor, the human resources representative for the North American operations of a large oil company, was a strong advocate of the role of the manager in employee retention and wanted to introduce practices and measurements to hold managers more accountable. During exit interviews she added several questions regarding how departing employees viewed their manager: "Did your manager show interest and support in your professional growth and development?" "Did your manager understand and utilize your preferred skills and strengths?" "Did you see your manager as a resource and support?"

Even though people might hesitate to express dissatisfaction when leaving a company for fear of burning bridges, over the course of 18 months, Taylor was able to document and champion the need to improve the management practices within the company.

Ask Questions and Listen Between the Lines

Once you are alert to the role of personal agendas—open or hidden— you are ready to develop a strategy for dealing with controversy and differences. The first step is to gather as much understanding as possible about others' points of view. This means that you ask a lot of questions and *really listen* to the answers.

Put yourself in the other person's shoes and let go of any preconceived notions. It's not necessary, in the early stages, to immediately reveal your point of view when it is different than theirs. Rather, seek more information and clarification about other people's thinking and how they arrived at the conclusions they did.

Even with a hidden or stated agenda, there is usually a rationale for endorsing a particular approach or course of action that you should consider independent of the personal need. Remember, personal and company wins can often be in alignment with one another, so you do not want to dismiss an idea solely because it also serves some additional personal purpose.

Explore the Other Person's Point of View

Being savvy about hidden agendas does not mean that you always assume that there is one. When you are listening closely to someone's suggestions and seeking to understand his or her reasoning, look for the logic and rationale. This alone might enable you to adopt his or her point of view, whether or not it serves a hidden agenda.

The way you go about exploring someone's thinking is critical to an effective result. You do not want to sound judgmental or confrontational. You want the other person to feel comfortable sharing his or her ideas and to be open with you about how he or she arrived at them. If the person feels criticized or interrogated, he or she will become defensive and guarded. In addition to watching what you say, be careful of how you say it. Your body language and tone of voice should also be neutral and nonargumentative.

You can open the discussion with a comment such as "I think that is a very interesting way of looking at the problem. Tell me how you arrived at that conclusion." During the other person's explanation, ask questions only for clarification to help you better understand their thought process, instead of offering your own comments and observations. Whenever appropriate—and sincere—provide your colleague with positive feedback, such as "what a unique observation," or "that's a very creative approach." Even if you do not agree with the conclusion, you can appreciate his or her process of reaching it.

The more you can encourage someone to speak freely, the more you can learn about their thinking; sometimes they might even hint at or reveal an agenda that was previously hidden. By encouraging others to talk, probing, and refraining from judging or offering your opinion in response, you can gather valuable information to guide you toward the best possible course of action.

Questions to Ask

The questions you ask can either encourage someone to be forthcoming or discourage him or her from doing so. Questions that demonstrate listening, interest in the other person's thinking, and respect for his or her thought processes are the most effective in getting others to open up.

Here are some examples of probing, open-ended questions that indicate interest without challenging another person's thinking or point of view:

+ "What do you think are the most important things to consider in order to achieve the best possible outcome?"

+ "What risks do you think we should avoid? What risks do you think we should be willing to take?"

+ "How did you decide to approach the issue from that angle?"

+ "Have you ever been in a similar situation in the past? What happened? How is this situation the same as what you've dealt with before? How is it different?"

+ "Did you think about approaching the issue another way? What led you to decide this was a better approach?"

Virtual Alert

Such exchanges should be face-to-face if possible; and if not, they should take place over the phone. You do not want to risk someone mistaking your questions for attacks. You want to avail yourself of the benefit of all the nonverbal feedback you can get: tone of voice, inflection, body language, and so on.

Also, if the other person is feeling somehow criticized or challenged, he or she might tend to be overcautious in their response, thus limiting the information you get, and perhaps causing them to feel that you are taking up an inordinate amount of their time.

Carefully Evaluate All Angles and Options

Once you have gathered as much information as you can, you need to weigh all the dynamics and consider the pros and cons for each of your options. There is no set formula for determining the best course of action, but being as clear and objective as possible will help guide you in the right direction.

Identify What Is at Stake for Others

As noted in the preceding section, figuring out others' agendas might not always be possible. When it is, you can assess how important and deeply valued a particular gain is to the person or persons involved. If someone has a lot riding on the outcome, and there is no compelling reason not to follow her or his approach or suggestions, going along might be the most prudent thing to do.

Also, this can be a great relationship-building opportunity. If you have discussed a person's agenda with him or her, you can indicate your desire to support this person in achieving his or her win.

Appreciate the Care and Feeding of Hidden Agendas

As I have already discussed, in many cases, people with hidden agendas are unaware of what is motivating their thinking. People often go to great lengths to reconfigure their agendas as something that is good for—or even urgently needed by—the company. And this by itself is by no means cause for condemnation or grounds for disregarding their projects or suggestions. Quite the opposite; this is a good reason to give their viewpoint every benefit of the doubt.

By the time someone takes a stand about an approach to a project, a solution to a problem, or an opportunity for the company, he or she has likely metamorphosed it from a personal need or desire to "the only way to go." When making their position public, they actually increase their stakes because their ego comes into play. They measure their power, credibility, and influence by whether others endorse their thinking. Thus, their investment continues to grow.

When people are coming from a hidden agenda, it can be extremely dicey to push too hard. Think very carefully about how you act in these situations, staying mindful that if the other person has more power, it is highly unlikely that anything you say will change his or her mind. And even if you can successfully argue for and implement your approach, ask yourself whether you can risk the continuing resentment of the other.

Consider Worst-Case Scenarios

It is best to be clear about exactly what is motivating you to champion your idea over someone else's. Outside of coming from your own agenda, there are other reasons—good reasons—to suggest different ways to approach a project or deal with a problem.

You might have had more experience in similar situations than the other people involved and are therefore confident that your way is better or more effective. Perhaps your solution is more efficient or cost-effective. You do not need to refrain from introducing your thoughts; in fact, you might be duty-bound to do so. You must, however, decide when to stop and compromise or acquiesce.

Ask yourself what's the worst that could happen: if you persist and win out, if you persist and get overruled, if you compromise, or if you give in. Take into consideration the power structure and future dealings with the individual or individuals involved. Think about what happens if your way is adopted and does not prove successful, or is sabotaged by the others.

Ignore These Thoughts!

If you find these thoughts running through your mind, don't listen to them!

✦ "I know John is coming from his own agenda and I'm going to call it to his attention in no uncertain terms."

✦ "I want to learn this new software and this might be my only chance. I have to bring the others around to my point of view."

✦ "I don't care what's motivating Sally to take such a strong position. I have the authority to make this decision and I'm going to do what I think is best."

Certainly there will be situations where perseverance is the only choice. You need to be quite vocal when indisputable technical realities predict certain product failure, a potential safety hazard, or a substantial loss of customer confidence. You want to be sure you are heard if you are reasonably certain that a particular direction will lead to unwanted or unintended consequences for individuals or the company.

Should you decide that you must push back because of the potentially negative consequences, and are dealing with a hidden agenda, do not do battle with the disguise. There is a very low probability that you will successfully win over another by arguing about the data and reasoning that led the person to a particular conclusion.

Instead, come at the issue from an entirely different angle. Do not address the other person's reasoning, but rather speak to the potentially negative consequence for the company, and therefore for them, if their preferred course of action is pursued. When you are dealing with a hidden agenda, the best way to sway opinion is if the potential loss for the other person is greater than the potential gain—no matter what that gain might be.

Choose the Appropriate Venue

If after carefully defining and evaluating the consequences, you feel you must pursue an issue further, it is important to do so as gently and privately as possible with the people concerned. When there is more than one person involved, you might want to talk to them as a group or to each of them, one at a time. If you choose to do the latter, be careful that it does not look like you are doing so in order to manipulate the situation. Be sure to disclose to each that you have talked, or intend to talk, with the others.

Don't "surprise" people with your intentions. Approach each person and disclose that you have some issues you want to discuss further and set up a convenient time to do so.

> *Charles was participating on a task force to identify the best software for a complex global accounting system for an international paper manufacturer. He had previous experience on a similar project with*

another company and experienced numerous problems with the particular software program that was endorsed by Fran, the project lead.

When Charles brought up his concerns, Fran was quick to push back. It was apparent to Charles that she had something at stake, even though he could not discover what that might be. After careful evaluation, he decided he was obliged to pursue the matter further. He diligently documented the problems from the previous project, in addition to gathering information from other users that corroborated his experience.

At a meeting of the task force, he presented the results of his thorough research, along with the consequences to the company if their experience with the software was similar to that of others. The team was seemingly left with no choice but to abandon its original direction and continue its search for a more suitable system.

Charles felt that he had done his job without bias, in a professional manner and in the best interest of the company. And indeed he had. Fran, however, felt that he stepped on her professional toes. She was well connected and respected throughout the company and in a position to influence how Charles was perceived. She honestly felt embarrassed and undermined by Charles and did not hide that she thought him to be a "know-it-all," a backstabber, and someone not to be trusted.

Charles was correct in his decision to pursue the matter. Actually, it was in Fran's best interest to select a different product if her decision would have proved costly in terms of efficiency, time, and money. Surely if she saw the result of his research, she would have realized the negative impact on her if she did not reverse her position. Charles' fatal mistake was neglecting to take up the matter with her in private so that it could be introduced to the team in a way that could enable Fran to save face.

Charles should have approached Fran after the meeting and stated, "I can see why you are attracted to this program. I was, too, when I was with my previous company. However, we experienced some real problems and I'm concerned that it will reflect badly on all of us if we don't take them into consideration. May I share them with you?"

Fran would have been hard pressed to deny him an audience. When Charles presented his case, he should have continually reinforced that the bugs were not readily apparent, thus making it logical that Fran would endorse the software.

Don't Make Someone Else "Wrong"

When presenting your perspective or concerns about another's ideas or preference, be sure to do so in a way that does not reflect poorly on their thought processes or competence. In the preceding example, Charles not only made public what should have been private, but he went about it in a way that could only be interpreted, at best, as questioning the ability and judgment of the lead.

The best way to present your thoughts or express concern about someone else's idea is to base your initial comments on what about their idea made sense and was well thought out. Acknowledge their ideas and expertise, and the value of their previous experiences. Point out how this particular situation differs and the implications for this specific instance. Emphasize that you want to make the team and everyone on it successful, and ask for feedback on the other person's reactions.

Then once again, really listen, and acknowledge the viability of the other person's thinking. Don't let the conversation turn into one where all of your sentences start with some version of "yes, but." If you sense this is about to happen, give it a rest. There is always a point at which it's time to give up.

If you are absolutely positive that the other person, team, or company is heading for certain and complete disaster, the most you can do is to tactfully say so and at the same time, express your willingness to support the others no matter what is decided.

Remember the Importance of Consensus and Cooperation

Perhaps you find yourself in a position that enables you to call the shots or influence others by virtue of your power. When you think you have the best answer, it is tempting to make a unilateral decision or disregard the suggestions and concerns of others. However, if you rely on those people to make your idea work, be careful about doing so.

The enthusiasm and ownership of those responsible for making something happen are critical to achieving the best possible results. Even if others are mandated toward a certain solution or direction, they can—consciously or subconsciously—sabotage the outcome. Sometimes everyone is better served if you are willing to be swayed in a direction other than the one you would chose in order to win the cooperation of all.

> CAUTION: *This does not mean that you acquiesce when you are certain that others are endorsing a course of action that will not bring about the desired results—or worse, that undermines the company. However, even in those cases, it is best to negotiate your way to consensus rather than dictate. Use the methods described in the preceding sections to make sure that everyone feels included and can get on board.*

Be Willing to Be Mistaken

Whenever opinions differ, it is extremely important that you be absolutely willing to admit that you might be off the mark in how you assess any situation or conceive any solution. This should be apparent in your attitude, your approach, and your words.

This posture is your most effective guarantee that both the best solution is found for the company and that you do not alienate your colleagues. It allows you to listen more carefully to others' viewpoints because you are not distracted by your own need to prove that you are right and your way is the best. And it encourages others to listen closely to you because they do not feel unduly pressured to see things your way.

Others appreciate knowing that they are heard and their viewpoints are respected. If you are open to the fact that you are fallible and might not see everything clearly, you are more likely to communicate your interest in and regard for the opinions of others. This does not suggest that you show a lack of confidence in yourself or that you blow whichever way the wind takes you. It simply means that you are open to the possibility that others might have a better idea or that you might be misguided in any particular situation.

Banish the thoughts "I told you so," "I knew it," and the like from your brain and never let those words escape your lips. Even if you warned that a course of action would prove problematical…even if you went to extraordinary lengths to get your point of view across…even if others dismissed you without much consideration, if a particular approach does not prove successful, you take the responsibility with everyone else. And conversely, you share the credit with everyone else if they adopt your idea and it is successful.

Be Aware of Your Own Agenda

To this point, I have addressed the agendas of others without pointing out that you are quite likely to have your own. You definitely want to be aware of how to leverage work situations to meet your own career goals and personal needs for satisfaction.

Having said that, be careful not to become so focused on your own agenda that you disregard everything else. The first step in maintaining the proper perspective is to be absolutely clear on your own agenda from the beginning. Know what your career goals are and how you can leverage work situations in order to meet them. Take stock up front so that your agendas don't become disguised to the point that you lose sight of what they are.

Then when you find yourself in a position to promote your own personal and professional interests, ask yourself first what would be best for the company or the situation. If the answer is in alignment with your own needs, you can proceed in that direction. If not, you are better off in the long run to consider alternatives that better serve the needs of the business. People who recklessly pursue a course of action only for the purpose of meeting their own needs eventually come to rue the practice. Be careful not to let your own gains become so compelling that you either fail to take into account all relevant data—or even worse, impede progress or undermine the ultimate results.

Try to avoid defenses such as the following:

+ Not listening to comments or suggestions

+ Getting emotional—sometimes spun as "passionate"—when talking about your point of view

+ Being inflexible or unresponsive

+ Sounding like a broken record

+ Giving evasive or irrational responses

+ Changing the subject

You are sure to find yourself in some situations in which your colleague's agenda is at cross purposes with your own. The first thing to determine is which direction or solution will promote the business' success. All things being equal, there is no easy answer for how to proceed. Perhaps you can negotiate a win-win-win solution where the company and all parties come out ahead. When this is not an option, carefully weigh all the issues before deciding on a course of action. Consider the importance of the relationships involved and what you stand to lose if you staunchly champion your solution. Carefully assess your point of view to ensure that, in your zeal, you are not overlooking important issues. Perhaps there is another opportunity where you can further your goals without stepping on a colleague's needs.

Again, whether to push forward or acquiesce is a judgment call. Sometimes the best way to proceed might not be easy to determine. When the answers are not clear, the best you can do is be sure that you are honest with yourself about your own agenda and aware of those of the others involved, always keeping in mind what best serves the company. Even when you are in a position to "win" (to successfully promote a direction that best serves your own agenda), the cost of doing so might not be worth it.

Recall in the Introduction when I discussed how people like to be right just because it feels good. Make sure that the need to be right is not your motivation to persist in your argument for your point of view. It will never serve you to take any stand just because you want to be right.

Reality Check: How Are You Doing?

Before you get into a position where you have to determine how to handle any difference of opinion, ask yourself the following questions:

+ What are the needs, goals, and personal and professional interests of those I routinely collaborate with? How do I know?

+ What are my needs, goals, and professional interests? How am I currently meeting them? How do I anticipate meeting them in the future? What kinds of opportunities get me closer to my goals?

If you are involved in a situation in which your viewpoint differs from another's, use the following questions as a tool to decide how to proceed. Let your answers guide you toward a course of action that promises the best outcome for you, the team, and the company.

+ What is the best possible outcome for the company? What is the best possible outcome for me?

+ Do I have a personal agenda? If so, what is it? Does my agenda support what is also good for the company?

+ Do others have their own agendas? What are they?

+ Is there a way I can help them realize their needs in a way that is also good for the company?

+ Is there a win-win-win in this where everyone gets what they want and the company also benefits?

✦ If another's direction will hurt the company, how can I proceed without making them "wrong" or stepping on their toes?

✦ What are the risks versus the possible gains if I continue to lobby for what I think is best?

✦ Can I really influence others to change direction or am I fighting a losing battle?

LISTEN BETWEEN THE LINES

Feedback Comes in Many Forms

I t is essential that you have a clear and accurate understanding of how you are perceived throughout the organization. This includes how you are regarded by your boss, your boss's boss, peers, customers and all others with whom you come in contact.

In school you had clear and concise feedback as to how you were doing in the form of your report cards and standardized test scores. In the world of work, the process is not so simple or straightforward. The formal system of feedback (performance reviews and 360-degree assessments) does not necessarily tell the whole story. You need to seek feedback based on the way people behave toward you. Often, you need to ask for direct feedback from people who are in a position to offer it.

Performance Appraisals Alone Aren't Enough

Most organizations have a structured methodology to provide feedback on the quality of your work, usually in the form of a performance review or appraisal. This is a structured and documented process involving communication of expectations, some type of rating or measurement, and written feedback with suggestions for continuing professional development. It usually takes place between you and your manager, and typically happens on an annual basis, but can occur more frequently. The review becomes part of your permanent record and is typically linked to pay raises and bonuses.

Considering the time, expense, and effort that a company invests in the process, it is reasonable to assume that your performance appraisal gives you all the information you need about how you are doing, and accurately reflects your value to the company. However, that is not necessarily the case. Although the concept of performance reviews seems good in theory, the information they provide gets skewed by the way the process is applied.

This does not mean that your review is of no use at all or that it is always inaccurate. Depending on the organization, performance reviews can be a useful tool to gauge your progress and direct your professional growth. However, given the potential flaws in the system, you don't want to rely *solely* on your performance appraisal for the feedback you need to assess how you are perceived in your company.

The Various Purposes of Performance Reviews

The purpose of performance reviews is not always clear and well articulated. Are they for the benefit of the employee so that he or she can continually develop and grow? Are they designed for the benefit of the company in order to achieve better business results? Are they a tool to provide documentation necessary to justify raises and bonuses? Are they there to provide protection against litigation and mitigate compensatory damages? Or are they a combination of all of these?

If the organization is unclear about the purpose and the application in the company, those doing the reviews will also be uncertain as to what is required of them. If this is the case, it cannot always be assumed that the resulting data correctly reflects the employee's performance. Even when the organization publicly states the objective of performance appraisals, a close examination of how they are completed and utilized is not always consistent with the public statement.

The Emotion Factor

The performance review process stirs up emotions. Because the process is prescribed, structured, and documented, it is, by definition, one of judgment. And it is part of your permanent file with implications for your compensation and, perhaps, success in the company. Performance appraisals bring out emotions and create tension in both you and the manager. It is easy to forget that the process should be one of constructive feedback and education.

The Managerial Information Gap

Managers do not always know the complexities of the job. The manager must fully understand your job in order to provide meaningful feedback. It is not at all unusual for him or her to be lacking all of the necessary information to accurately evaluate your performance.

Just One Person's Opinion

Often the review is only the manager's perception. Therefore, the appraisal might be skewed in terms of how you are seen by others in the company. Managers are not necessarily required to gather information from others internal or external to the company. Therefore, your review might not reflect how customers, direct reports, peers, and other management see you. This holds true whether your appraisal is glowing or cites the need for improvement.

Unskilled Reviewers

Managers are often not adequately skilled in the conduct of performance appraisals. A truly effective appraisal requires that the manager gather the necessary data and prepare for the meeting. He or she must know how to involve and engage you in the process. For the appraisal to be truly useful, the manager needs to get your viewpoint, probe to understand your perspective on your performance, and offer actionable guidance on how to improve. Even when an action plan is required, many managers do not know how to create one that is specific, realistic, and measurable.

Also, many managers are reluctant to provide constructive feedback. Because of this, they tend to distort or tone down their communication of deficient performance.

Infrequency of Reviews

Appraisals usually take place once or twice a year at most. This can be interpreted to mean that feedback need not be continual and ongoing. Many managers forget that the most useful feedback is offered immediately after a behavior or situation. If offered long after the event, memory is often distorted and inaccurate on the part of both parties, thus making the feedback essentially meaningless in terms of providing a platform for improvement.

The Paper Problem

Performance reviews rely heavily on forms. Thus, the form becomes the review. The focus is on the completion of the form rather than meaningful and actionable communication between two people.

Additionally, appraisals are documented. This amplifies a hesitation to tell you where you might be underperforming. Many people are uncomfortable going on the record about what they consider to be bad news.

360-Degree Feedback Assessments

To provide their employees with broader feedback to use for professional development, many companies offer some sort of 360-degree feedback assessment. This usually automated tool provides you with feedback from people who routinely interact with you, including your supervisor, peers, direct reports, coworkers, and customers. Although this gives you more information than your performance review about how others view you, there are still drawbacks to this methodology in terms of its ability to provide accurate and actionable information:

+ **The skills and behaviors on which you are rated are predetermined.** There are many ways to go about determining the competencies for a 360-degree tool, and some are more strategic and targeted than others. However, no matter how the items are selected, there are probably other important behaviors, activities, and skills about which you are not getting feedback.

+ **The skills and behaviors on which you are rated are not necessarily directly linked to the competencies required for your specific job.** Often the items on which you are rated result from a software tool being used on a broad scale throughout the company. They do not directly address your job or what is important in your particular function or department. This usually leaves you with too much information and no meaningful way to use it.

+ **The feedback can be confusing or insufficient.** Because the process is anonymous, you have no way of clarifying and understanding the feedback. For example, say you are rated as "needing improvement" in your presentation skills. You have no way of knowing exactly where and how you are falling short. The problem could be with your preparation, organization, clear communication, or delivery style to name a few. Without this kind of information, it is difficult to act on the feedback.

+ **Comments rarely provide enough clarification for action.** Even when a rater takes the time to elaborate on an item by including a comment, it quite often is not sufficient to provide the information necessary to take relevant action. And again, the feedback is anonymous, so you cannot pursue it further with the person who gave it.

+ **The feedback can be inconsistent.** Your ratings on any item can vary greatly from rater to rater, making it virtually useless because you have no means of clarification.

+ **Raters often have their own agendas.** Raters, even though they are told they are anonymous, might fear retribution and therefore hesitate to be honest in their evaluation. Or they might want to make you look good—or bad. There is really no way to know whether your ratings are skewed.

+ **Raters are inexperienced or untrained.** Even if raters have no personal agendas, they often do not have sufficient training to know how to rate you.

This does not mean that you should discount or disregard 360-degree feedback. The information *can* give you some understanding of how you are doing in your job, and you can use it to direct your development planning and goal setting. It is also important to respond because there is authority behind it and the expectation that you will act on it. However, it doesn't necessarily provide you with the whole picture. You need to seek other sources of feedback to ensure that you have a complete and accurate understanding of how you are perceived throughout your company.

Feedback as a Gift

Feedback, when it's part of a structured system, mandated by the organization, and recorded and part of your permanent record, loses some of its value as accurate and actionable information. The reason is that it is partially or fully "owned" by the company. Such formal systems are used to determine compensation, bonuses, and promotions. As such, they can be perceived as evaluative, judgmental, and a measure of your worth. Even in organizations that intend formal feedback to be developmental and an opportunity for growth, the very formality hinders it from being entirely experienced that way.

Another kind of feedback is information offered with no evaluation or immediate consequence in terms of a formal, far-reaching reward or penalty. You totally own it and its only purpose is to let you know whether your behavior is moving you toward your goals. This type of feedback allows you to get back on track before there are any unintended or undesirable consequences of your actions. It prevents you from being blindsided after it's too late to do anything to correct or redirect your efforts.

This feedback, therefore, needs to be informal, private, and for your use only, to do with as you will. It has no direct impact on your salary or any other rewards and allows you to correct your behavior before it has any lasting negative effect on your success.

Feedback offered for your use only is a gift. It presents you with information that you might otherwise be unaware of and it does so in enough time to remedy or mitigate any long-range consequence. It provides you with the chance to impact the future, whereas formal feedback, even though it is also an opportunity for improvement, is documented and becomes part of your record.

Obtaining accurate and meaningful informal feedback is a skill that can be learned. Feedback is available directly in what people tell you, and indirectly in how they behave toward you. The rest of this chapter tells you how to look for it, ask for it, and respond to it.

Indirect Feedback Is Everywhere

You can glean invaluable information by becoming sensitive to how others relate to you. Often, once you learn to read it, this is the purest and most accurate source of feedback. It occurs in real-time. And although people might measure what they say, most cannot disguise body language and tone of voice. Therefore, indirect feedback does not so easily lend itself to tweaking and editing on the part of the giver.

The following circumstances illustrate how the behavior and comments of others might be considered as feedback. A single circumstance, when taken alone, is of relatively little importance. Look for trends and patterns. When similar behaviors and events happen repeatedly, they probably hold valuable information for you.

+ **Your peers and supervisor frequently seek your assistance in solving technical problems.** This can be taken to mean that they think you have strong technical skills and respect your opinion on such matters.

+ **Your presence is not obvious or memorable.** You are on a task force to select accounting software. Referring to the last session, the team lead remarks, "I forgot that you were at that meeting." This probably means that your participation and contribution at that particular meeting were negligible, at least insofar as the lead is concerned.

+ **Your reputation precedes you.** You are called by a colleague whom you have never met, located in another city. She tells you she has heard that you have completed a project similar to one that has just been assigned to her and she wants to learn how you handled it. This tells you that your work was considered to be high quality and the project was successful. It also means that the word is getting around the company.

✦ **People don't make eye contact with you.** You notice that during a discussion among you and several colleagues, whoever is speaking does not make eye contact with you. You can conclude that you are not considered to have power or valuable input in the conversation.

Look for More Subtle Forms of Feedback

Silence can be the loudest form of indirect feedback. Because people are generally hesitant to express negative comments, concerns, or disappointments, especially without an open invitation to do so, they might say nothing at all. Although this isn't always the case, you should always note and investigate silence to determine whether important information is behind it.

Body language and tone of voice speak louder than words. People can more easily edit what they say than they can their posture or tone of voice. If their words are not consistent with the latter, don't place too much credence in their words.

Once you attune yourself to the subtle—and sometimes not-so-subtle—behavior of colleagues, you can learn a great deal about how they perceive you.

Often you will need to do a reality check about how you interpret someone's behavior or comments, especially when what they say or do might be out of character. Also, remember that another's behavior is not always about us. Rather, he or she might be preoccupied, having a bad day, or deliberately flattering you because they see you in a position of power.

Action Items

☐ Identify situations, past and future, where indirect feedback is available to you, and make a list of what it might mean.

☐ Think of direct feedback you have already received and note whether it is consistent with the indirect feedback you've observed.

Indirect Feedback Is Open to Many Interpretations

There are many circumstances that, although they contain feedback for you, are open to several different interpretations. It can be misleading and potentially harmful to assume what something might mean without doing a reality check.

The following examples illustrate that multiple meanings can be assigned to a single event.

✦ You complete a half-hour presentation and ask for questions and comments. There are many questions regarding how you arrived at your conclusions and how you obtained your data. This could mean that people are suspect of the content of the presentation and want to be absolutely certain that it was based on reliable, valid information. Or it could be interpreted to mean that they absolutely trusted your conclusion but were not as astute on the subject as you, so they needed further explanation. Another possibility is that you were not clear and organized in the way you presented the data.

✦ You are not asked to participate on a project similar to those you have worked on before. It is possible that your previous contributions were not considered valuable. Or it might have nothing to do with you and could simply mean that your manager wanted to give other people an opportunity to get this kind of experience. Another possibility is that you are being saved for something bigger and better coming just around the corner.

✦ You make a suggestion at a staff meeting and it is essentially glossed over. Someone else presents a similar idea and it is greeted with interest and enthusiasm. Perhaps you didn't present your idea clearly, or your peers don't really listen to you or respect your opinion. It is also possible that they needed to hear the idea again or stated differently before it really took hold.

✦ Your direct reports check in with you every step of the way when they are working on a special project you assign them. You could take this to mean that you did not clearly communicate your expectations. Or perhaps you have not let them know that you have confidence in their ability to do the project well. Or perhaps this means that you are seen as a micromanager or needing everything done your way. Another possibility is that they have high regard for you and value your expertise and opinions.

In the preceding situations, you need to get direct feedback to understand the meaning of other people's behavior. Often, sufficient information from prior circumstances lends credibility to one particular interpretation over another.

In the first situation, if you have prior feedback and experience to suggest that you understand your subject in much greater depth than most people and others recognize your expertise, you can conclude that the many questions were an attempt to learn from you. In the last example, if you have received comments and observations from others that you are a micromanager, it is safe to assume that it is that perception that is driving your direct reports' behavior. There is no need to question people in order to understand their behavior. However, in the absence of such data, it behooves you to further investigate what message is contained in others' behavior.

Virtual Alert

Noticing and interpreting indirect feedback during the exchange of e-mails and conference calls presents a unique challenge, especially if you have had little or no opportunity for face-to-face encounters with the person or persons involved. You are lacking a great deal of information to help you interpret what their words or tone might be telling you.

Before contacting these people to validate what might constitute feedback, accumulate data from several virtual interactions. If their behavior is consistent over several contacts, and you do not know them other than from a distance, you must broach the conversation carefully.

Begin with an e-mail that invites them to set up a time when you can converse over the phone. Explain that you would like to get their perspective on how effective they think your working relationship with them is. Put them at ease by saying that you value their perspective and want to make sure that you are supporting them.

When you talk with them, refer to the behaviors you have noticed without judgment or accusation. Explain that you are checking in with them because you want to make sure you understand the message behind their behavior, if indeed there is one. Let them know that if there is meaning behind their behavior, you want to understand what it might be so that you can support them and make a greater contribution in your role. Invite them to initiate any feedback that they might have for you in the future.

Resist the urge to disregard or shrug off a particular situation rather than seek additional feedback. Although not everything that happens is significant, it is better to start with the assumption that something is worth looking at and find out otherwise, than to ignore circumstances that offer you valuable feedback and a chance to act on it.

Ignore These Thoughts!

If you find these thoughts running through your mind, don't listen to them!

✦ "I'm sure that Judy's silence when I challenged her viewpoint didn't mean anything. She's probably just having a bad day."

✦ "I'm not going to worry about not getting copied on e-mails about the conversion. I'm sure it's just an oversight."

✦ "My colleagues are always disregarding my suggestions because they are jealous of my success."

CAUTION: In your efforts to notice and validate indirect feedback, do not overinterpret behavior or check in on everything a person says or does. Compile data from many contacts and also consider other direct feedback you have previously received. This alone might give you the information you need. You don't want to take up an inordinate amount of people's time, nor appear so sensitive that people feel scrutinized and that they need to watch everything they say and do around you.

Demonstrate Your Receptivity to Feedback

There are essentially two broad categories of feedback: that which concerns your work, and information about your habits, style, and interpersonal qualities. Sometimes the latter impacts the former, and sometimes not.

Both types of information are critical to your success. If you do exceptional work but are considered unpleasant and difficult to work with, eventually you will run into the consequences. Conversely, if you are considered a delight to be around, but produce substandard work, you will in time run into stumbling blocks.

When seeking feedback, you want to ask for both kinds. Often, it is easier to request and accept feedback about our work than about ourselves.
It is also more comfortable for people to offer feedback about what you
produce than it is to address personal issues and behaviors. It's *your* job
to put people at ease with giving both kinds of information. You want
to make it easy for others by the way you interact with them on a daily
basis, approach them to ask for specific feedback, and receive and react
to the observations and opinions they offer.

Your receptivity to feedback will influence the quality of the information people are willing to offer. The greater the extent that you are
viewed as open and approachable, the more likely you are to get honest
feedback. This means that your effort to obtain quality feedback is an
ongoing process that actually begins from your first interactions with
people, before you ever actually ask them for specific feedback.

Your goal is to make people comfortable around you. You want them to
feel that you are easy to talk to, a good listener, and interested in them.
These are the qualities that put people at ease around you. You want to
do everything you can to ensure that you are getting honest feedback.
Anything less defeats the purpose of asking for it at all.

Tips for Being Approachable

There are some things you can do deliberately, whether you are
extremely extroverted or very shy, to be seen as approachable and lay the
groundwork for receiving feedback at some future time:

+ Ask people about themselves and really listen. People feel more
  comfortable around those who have shown an interest in them.

+ Offer help and encouragement to others. They will come to regard
  you as a resource and a partner and are more willing to be the same
  for you.

+ Reveal "benign" information about yourself. Tell people about
  your hobbies, interests, and past work experience. People relate
  more openly to others they feel they know.

✦ Talk about past mistakes and what you learned from them. This demonstrates that you know you are not perfect and are comfortable and open to learning from your mistakes.

✦ Watch your own indirect feedback. Just as you are receiving indirect feedback from everyone, you are also sending it. Make sure that you are sending out the signals you intend to. Be aware of your body language, tone of voice, and eye contact. Others will take such behavior personally whether or not it is any reflection on them.

✦ Be willing to offer valuable feedback. If people have received useful feedback from you, they are more inclined to do the same for you.

Nine Criteria for Giving Useful Feedback in Return

The way you give feedback models the way you want to receive it. The ongoing exchange of feedback between two people constitutes a mutually valuable relationship. Be sure that you meet the nine criteria for giving useful feedback:

1. **It is welcome.** Unless someone directly requests feedback, ask whether he or she wants it pertaining to a specific situation or behavior. "I am wondering if you would like some feedback on the way you reacted to Sally during the meeting."

2. **It is descriptive, not evaluative.** It focuses on behaviors and includes examples. "When she was speaking, you folded your arms and were silent, and then asked if anyone else had any thoughts."

3. **It acknowledges what works as well as what doesn't.** "You really were attentive while she was talking and made good eye contact. But then you moved on without seeming to have considered her thoughts, as though nothing was said."

4. **It is specific, related to a definite occurrence the receiver can understand and relate to.** "At last week's staff meeting, in discussing the new 360-degree feedback tool, Jeffrey suggested that the process might be more effective if the reports did not go into the employee's permanent personnel file. You thanked him for his comments and acknowledged that raters might be hesitant to be totally honest. Then you moved on to the next agenda item without addressing the validity and value of his suggestion."

5. **It is actionable.** The receiver can do something about the behavior the feedback addresses. "It would encourage people to offer their ideas and suggestions if you did or said something to indicate that their input was appreciated, even if not acted upon. You might invite them to elaborate, indicate that you will take their thought into consideration and get back to them, or express why you cannot change anything."

6. **It is well timed.** Feedback is most useful at the earliest opportunity after the given behavior, or just prior to when the person is likely to repeat the behavior.

7. **It is clear.** Rephrase and summarize the feedback; then ask the receiver to repeat what he or she heard.

8. **It is truthful.** It accurately reflects your perception.

9. **It is offered in an objective, nonemotional fashion with positive intent.** In other words, it is meant to be useful to the receiver, not a way for you to express anger or further a personal agenda.

Distinguish Between Feedback and a Request

You must be aware of whether you are offering feedback solely for the benefit of the recipient or whether you have a stake in the issue being addressed. Feedback is the purest when you are not impacted by whether the individual takes any action on it. You have no stake in the consequence of the other person's behavior. Her or his work has no effect on anything you are involved with or on your success in the company. It is offered only because the other might benefit from it.

When the information is offered because you want someone to change her or his behavior, there is an added dimension. You provide your feedback because you want something to happen or stop happening as a result of it. Be aware that it is more likely for emotions to surface on both sides, and take steps to minimize the extent to which they muddy the waters.

For example, Sally has a habit of interrupting people and either offering her own ideas or finishing their sentences for them. This can inadvertently make others feel that she is not really listening and does not value their thoughts or opinions. You can point this out to Sally solely because you think it is useful to her to be aware of it; or, in addition, because you want her to quit interrupting you. Even though there is valuable information for Sally in both scenarios, you want to approach the conversation differently according to your stake in it.

In the latter case, ask Sally for permission to offer her feedback and let her know upfront that the behavior has an effect on you. "Sally, would you like some feedback on our discussion about the holiday party and my experience during it?"

After Sally agrees to hear your comments, make sure that you do not evaluate or judge, such as labeling her behavior as "rude" or "overbearing." If possible, introduce the topic from a positive perspective, such as in this example: "You have such good ideas and get so enthusiastic that it pumps me up, too. However, in your zeal, you often interrupt me before I can finish my thoughts. I would appreciate it if you let me complete my ideas before sharing yours."

Action Items

❏ Identify one or two people for whom you have relevant feedback.

❏ Prepare and practice before approaching them to offer your feedback.

Asking for and Receiving Feedback

You will be asking people to essentially do one of two things: to explain or validate indirect feedback—after the fact—or to observe and comment on a future event. The better someone understands the feedback you are seeking, the more useful he or she can be.

Selecting the Sources of Feedback

Everyone is potentially a provider of valuable feedback: colleagues, peers, direct reports, and internal and external customers. In selecting people to provide feedback in any specific situation, consider the following:

✦ **Does the giver have the background, experience and ability necessary to have meaningful input?** If you are preparing a presentation for a particular group, someone familiar with the members would have greater credibility than someone who was not. If you want feedback about your behavior at a meeting, someone who was present would have better information than someone who is hearing a second-hand account.

✦ **Will the giver feel free to be totally honest?** Sometimes the giver might have reason to edit or soften the feedback. This is partially under your control based on the past experiences of the giver in offering you feedback. If you've been appreciative and gracious, the giver will feel freer to tell you the truth. However, depending on whether you have any power over the giver, he or she might feel the need to be cautious. A direct report might have a tendency to soften or skew his or her feedback. An internal customer who relies on your prompt response to his or her needs might be hesitant to be fully forthcoming for fear you might not be as accommodating in the future.

+ **Does the giver want you to be successful?** If a peer sees you as a competitor for favor or resources, she or he might not be a reliable source.

+ **Is the giver free to provide you with the information you are seeking?** If giving you feedback represents any kind of conflict of interest or violation of confidence, the feedback might not be as "clean."

It's important to have several sources of direct feedback because it is unlikely that one individual will be able to provide you with the all feedback you need. Different people will have different stakes and perspectives. Also, you might behave differently with different people under different circumstances. You want to be able to choose feedback providers according to the particulars of any situation. It is your responsibility to seek, evaluate, and take action on feedback.

Be Specific

If you are an astute observer of indirect feedback, aware of your strengths and developmental needs, and clear about your goals, you should know what kind of information you are seeking. It is important that you be as specific as possible about what you are asking so that your feedback source can respond in a meaningful way.

Asking "How do you think my presentation went?" will not provide you with meaningful information in that it does not communicate the kind of observation and information you require. Also, it implies that you want the other person to evaluate your presentation as opposed to offering objective observations.

Try this instead:

> *I noticed that there were no questions or comments after my presentation. Did I ramble or did the information flow in a logical fashion?*

Did you notice whether the audience was engaged? Was I dynamic?
What suggestions can you offer so that I can improve next time?

The latter guides the other person and invites a discussion and mutual exploration of what the silence might have meant. It initiates a conversation that is interactive and engaging, and creates a partnership.

When you are asking for input on an upcoming situation, it is equally important to direct the observations and comments of the person from whom you are requesting feedback.

I know I get carried away and can sometimes talk too much at staff
meetings. I would really appreciate your help with this. Please be
alert to my behavior at the meeting this morning and give me feed-
back on whether my comments are relevant, to-the-point, and add
value. I'd like to know what suggestions are useful to the group and
which ones might be merely a by-product of my own enthusiasm.
Your insights would be really useful to me.

Notice the elements of the preceding request for feedback:

+ It is very specific about the information for which you are asking.

+ It acknowledges that the person asking is aware of this particular behavior.

+ It tells the person being asked that his or her observations are valuable and appreciated, thus laying the groundwork for honest feedback.

Understand and Ask for Both Constructive and Positive Feedback

Both kinds of feedback contain important information. Often, because of the emphasis on professional development, there is a disproportionate emphasis on areas where improvement is indicated. Although you want to be aware of what

(CONTINUED)

(CONTINUED)

you need to do to continuously improve at work, you want to be equally cognizant of your strengths. Effective professional development focuses not only on improving where you are weak, but also on growth in areas where you do very well. I will visit this again later in this chapter, when I talk about evaluating feedback.

Make sure you ask for and understand both. Most people often have "unconscious competence": things that they do very well but are not aware of what or how they do it. You can be very good at something and it seems so second nature and simple to you that you fail to appreciate that it is not common to everyone. Further, you might not understand exactly what it is that you do that makes you so good at whatever it is. Often, knowing what and why you are good at something is just as important to your success as knowing where you need to improve.

Remember That Feedback Is Never Wrong

This is a critical concept to keep in mind in order to receive and benefit from honest feedback. The information should always be regarded as truth in the eye of the beholder. Always assume that the person offering feedback is being honest about what he or she perceives and her or his reaction to it. Therefore, he or she is always telling the truth.

Given that, *never argue with feedback*. To do so is a guarantee that you will not get it again from the person with whom you are arguing. Remember, feedback is for your benefit. It is not to provide you with an opportunity to change the giver's mind. Unlike your performance review, there is no formal consequence of how the giver sees a particular behavior or situation. You should regard the perception and experience of another person as a piece of legitimate data. Because it is offered for your benefit only, it is up to you what you do with it. Of course, if the feedback is also a request for a change in your behavior, you want to make every effort to comply. In either case, there is nothing to be gained, and much to be lost, if you attempt to debate the validity of the feedback.

Do not explain or defend yourself. Resist the temptation to justify your behavior or clarify the thought process behind your actions. Again, feedback is for you to take in and evaluate. There is no need to initiate a lengthy conversation around it.

Ignore These Thoughts!

If you find these thoughts running through your mind, don't listen to them!

+ "She will see things differently when I explain what I was thinking."

+ "He doesn't understand me or he wouldn't have said that."

+ "I've tried doing it another way and it doesn't work for me. I will tell her about that and she will change her mind."

Accept Feedback Graciously

It is absolutely essential that you demonstrate your appreciation for feedback, or you can be sure you will cut off your supply. You never want anyone to feel punished for offering you feedback, and *anything* other than a grateful "thank you" will be experienced as just that.

That does not mean that you will not react emotionally to some feedback. In fact, the more surprised you are, the more unwelcome the news, and the more personal the feedback, the more likely that you will react emotionally.

Emotional reactions to feedback typically consist of the following stages, which I call the "dance around SARA."

+ **Shock:** When feedback isn't what you would want to hear or comes as a surprise, it is understandable that you would be taken aback. If the news is unexpected, it means that you were completely unaware of the behavior and its effect on people. The irony is that the more surprised you are, the greater the gift. Often it is these blind spots that can eventually come back to bite you. And when they do, you will be clueless as to why and therefore, prone to continue the self-defeating behaviors, styles, or habits.

✦ **Anger:** Once the shock wears off and the words sink in, anger is a predictable response. How dare so-and-so tell you something like this! They're really one to talk. In your anger, you might find all sorts of things wrong with the person who gave you the feedback.

✦ **Rebuttal:** There is frequently a tendency to find reasons why the feedback is "wrong." You might want to get back to the giver and explain why he or she was off base. Perhaps he or she really didn't understand why you behaved as you did. Surely if he or she knew the real reason, they would see things differently. Or you might be thinking that this person is out to get you. Perhaps they are jealous. You might search for whatever reason you can find to disqualify his or her perception.

✦ **Acceptance:** Once you get to this stage, you are comfortable with the idea that the feedback was true in the eyes of the giver. You are now ready to get back to him or her and ask any questions you might have. This is when you can objectively decide what actions, if any, you want to take in response to the feedback.

When you feel yourself reacting emotionally to feedback, simply say something to the giver like, "Thank you. I really appreciate your input." Get permission to seek them out later with any questions and remove yourself from the situation as quickly as possible. Although you want to honor your "dance around SARA," you do not want to make it public, nor do you want to determine how to respond in the throes of it.

If you know that you are distracted, stressed, or for whatever reason not receptive to feedback in a particular moment, negotiate another time to receive it. There is no reason to set yourself up by hearing feedback when you are quite likely to overreact and respond emotionally. You can simply say something like "I really value your feedback and want to learn from it. Right now, I have to get this other situation handled, so let me get back to you when I can give your comments my full attention."

At times you might get feedback that you did not ask for, nor do you want. It might be offered with language that is hurtful or even offensive. Unfortunately, many people are not skilled at giving feedback. It is nevertheless in your best interest to react to such situations with the same graciousness as you do when you invite the feedback.

Ask Questions to Clarify Feedback

Although you don't want anyone to feel that they have to defend their feedback, you do want to make sure you understand it. This means that you have to ask questions to clarify, and do so in a manner that does not sound argumentative or defensive.

For example, you are told that you went into too much detail when you presented an idea. You did so because you wanted to make sure that people had sufficient background to understand how you arrived at your conclusion. You are not sure how you could have gotten your idea across without giving all the background information.

If you phrase the question as *"Do you think they would have understood, given the complexity of the subject,"* it sounds like you are defending your behavior—or worse, making the giver wrong or naive. However, you might say "Help me understand what I could have left out and still offered enough background information." By responding his way, you are not making the giver wrong. Rather, you are asking for clarification and inviting the giver to collaborate with you.

Sometimes you might get feedback that is so different from your own internal experience of the situation that you simply don't understand it. You might be told that you seemed agitated during a meeting when you were actually feeling quite the opposite. You don't want to negate or disregard this information just because your own experience was different. Rather, you want to understand what you might have done to communicate agitation. When something like this happens, ask for specific behaviors or words that gave someone this impression. "Can you tell me exactly what I said or did that made me seem that way?"

Remember, when you get the answer, simply thank the other person. Do not make them wrong by saying something like, "Oh no. That isn't what I meant by that," or worse, "You read me all wrong." You might correct the perception by saying something like, "I really appreciate that information because that is not at all how I was feeling and I did not mean to give that impression." When you phrase it in this manner, you correct the other person's conclusion while still honoring his or her perspective.

You might sometimes get general feedback, such as, "Your last report was not up to your usual standards." Even if you think you know what they are referring to, make sure you are not missing anything by asking for specific examples.

The best time to ask questions is immediately after you are given feedback, while it is fresh in the giver's mind. You might think of some things later and you certainly want to make sure you are as clear as possible about the feedback. However, you do not want someone to feel that the feedback conversation is never-ending. Ask upfront if you can get back to them with further questions, and then compile a list so that you need contact them only once to get the remainder of the information you need to clarify their feedback.

Action Items

❐ From your list of indirect feedback, identify that which you would like validated or clarified.

❐ Determine who might be able to validate or clarify the feedback.

❐ Prepare succinct questions and schedule a time to talk with the feedback giver.

Evaluate Feedback

I have already discussed that feedback is always true to the person offering it, and it is not to be rebutted or debated. However, sometimes you will get varying or conflicting feedback from different people. Although each is telling his or her own truth, you need to determine whether a particular perception represents a majority view. This is yet another reason to have several sources of feedback.

Once you determine that a particular piece of feedback represents a majority perspective, you need to decide what action, if any, you want to take on it and how you will measure progress. Assess the importance of the issue to achieving your goals and determine the effort and time required to improve or change. Consider asking the people who offered the feedback whether they would be willing to provide it ongoing as you take corrective actions.

When feedback comes from your manager or is part of your performance review or documented through a 360-degree instrument, you most likely do not have a choice as to whether to act on it. It is when the feedback is offered for your use only that you can choose to stop the behavior, continue the behavior, or change the behavior.

Reward the Giver

There are many ways to reward those who give you the gift of feedback. In addition to thanking them, give details on how their comments were useful, such as, "I had no idea that my nervous gestures were so distracting. I am much more effective in meetings since you pointed that out."

Follow up to let someone know how you put his or her suggestions to use. An e-mail telling him or her that you followed the suggestions for your PowerPoint presentation and got rave reviews will be much appreciated.

Sometimes a small token or grateful gesture is called for. When someone took a big risk or offered you feedback that resulted in a triumph, a small gift or invitation to lunch is an appropriate demonstration of your gratitude. Don't make this a common practice; reserve it for truly special circumstances.

Reality Check: How Are You Doing?

Use the following questions to help you assess whether you have sufficient feedback to know how you are perceived and valued by your company:

+ Who are my primary sources of feedback? What about each makes this person a valid and valuable source?

+ Do I need to actively seek other sources of feedback?

+ Specifically what do I want feedback about?

+ What situations are coming up that I would like feedback about?

+ How well do I provide feedback to others? Do they appreciate it? How do I know?

+ What topics of feedback am I sensitive about? What do I do— or not do—in order to ensure I receive feedback on them?

+ What indirect feedback do I receive? Do I need to validate it? If so, with whom?

+ What feedback have I received that I want to take action on? Why?

+ What feedback have I received that I do not want to take action on? Why?

After answering each of the following questions, ask yourself, "How do I know?"

+ How does my boss see me?

+ How do my peers see me?

+ How do my direct reports see me?

+ How close am I to reaching my professional goals?

+ What skills, abilities, and talents of mine does the company value?

+ Where does the company perceive that I need to develop?

GET OVER YOURSELF

Being Valuable Doesn't Mean Being Indispensable

You've just been promoted, have been assigned to a prestigious task force, or have developed skills critical to the organization. You get continual feedback from a variety of sources to validate that you are a well-respected, valuable contributor. You have built relationships up, down, and across the organization. You have earned your colleagues' trust and confidence.

Further, you now have a certain degree of power. People are constantly seeking you out for your viewpoint. You notice that you can influence others' thoughts and behavior.

You might have power derived from where you sit on the org chart. You could control the allocation of resources, or have credibility with and access to those who do. Perhaps you have expertise and knowledge essential to the success of an important initiative.

Having paid your dues, it's only natural that you might expect to get cut some slack on occasion and enjoy the benefit of hard-earned perks. After all, having given your best and made significant contributions, it's about time that you can relax a bit and reap the rewards.

But it's just when you start to feel bullet proof that you need to be more cautious than ever. With increased success and responsibility comes increased visibility. So although some things might be more easily forgiven, some of what you did before without any ill consequences might now lead to negative repercussions.

The Brighter Your Star, the More Visible You Are

The reality is that you are more vulnerable than you were before you achieved this elevated status. Why? It's because you are more visible to more people in the company than ever before. People are watching you. The reasons they are watching you might vary from person to person, but what you do and say are more public, and thus more important, than they used to be.

You Are a Model

Some people will be observing you because they are aware of your stature in the company or department and they want to learn from you. They want to know how you got there so that they can do the same.

Perhaps they are new to the company and in the process of learning the culture. They assume your behavior reflects the organization's values and that by watching you they can learn how to also be successful.

You might be mentoring someone, either formally or informally, implicit or explicit. This individual is actually seeking and acting on your advice and deliberately using your behavior as a model for his or her own.

Someone Else's Success Depends on You

In many cases, you are where you are because others have endorsed or supported you. They have gone on record about their belief in your competence and ability to achieve a particular outcome. When someone goes to bat for you, his or her success is then linked to yours.

Good decision making and recognizing talent are vital components of success in any company, and if someone demonstrates weakness in either, it will hinder his or her progress. If you do not turn out to be everything that he or she promised, his or her career suffers. Once someone else has a stake in your performance, that person will watch you even more closely than before.

You Got What Someone Else Wanted

If others were vying for the same promotion, assignment, honor, level of achievement, or the like, they will be scrutinizing your every move to understand why you were chosen over them. They might be looking to learn from you, or they could be resentful. They could feel that you did not deserve what you got. And, sometimes, they might even be hoping that you trip and fall along the way. Whatever the case, they will be watching you and, possibly, harshly judging your every move.

You Talk to More People and They Talk More About You

As you move up in the organization and become known by more people, your visibility increases exponentially. Your name will come up more in conversations. There is no reason to think that the talk is anything other than positive; however, if you trip up the word will spread, and it will spread quickly. You do not want to be seen as taking undue advantage of your newly earned success, nor as less accessible than you once were. Perceptions such as these can attach themselves to your reputation to the point that you could eventually stumble over them.

You Are Being Evaluated for Future Opportunities

Once you get a reputation for being a valuable contributor, you become an asset to the company. The management above you is looking for ways to capitalize on your skills and talents. That means you are getting more attention from them. They are more closely watching and evaluating how you conduct yourself and what you produce.

Now, things that didn't matter before become potential stumbling blocks. This is not only because what you do is being observed more closely, but also because expectations are elevated. Therefore, it's just when you start to be valued and recognized that you become more vulnerable to stumbling into trouble than you ever anticipated. In fact, things that were formerly unimportant might take on new meaning.

If you haven't already been doing so, be mindful of your language. Even if others might use four-letter words, you are best to eliminate them from your vocabulary. Be careful. If you curse away from the office, the same words will slip out at work. Break yourself of the habit. Unless the culture requires cursing—and few do—you are best to refrain.

If you have been occasionally lax on dress or personal use of e-mail and phone, start paying attention to these things. Be careful not to talk negatively about others, or about company projects or practices. These kinds of comments might have not hurt you before, but you are in the limelight now and the attention calls for more, not less, thought and consideration to your professional behavior.

> ### Virtual Alert
>
> Don't deceive yourself into believing that geography in any way gives you more privacy or freedom from scrutiny than if everyone is on the same site. True, all parties will not be present to witness your every move. You are safest, however, to assume that everyone knows everything you do and everything you say. Although this will not be entirely accurate, you're better off behaving as though it is.

Watch Out for Those Obscure Boundaries

So many policies and practices of corporate life are not set forth in black and white. The work world is filled with shades of gray. You need to figure out for yourself what is alright and what is not. You will often find yourself in situations where there is no prescribed course of action and you must make a judgment call. Oh how wonderful it would be have "recipes" that you could follow to the letter and achieve a perfect outcome every time. That is not the case, however. What works in one company or department might lead to disaster in another. Even in the same company or department, the best choice can vary from situation to situation, from person to person.

Determining Boundaries

You can test and determine boundaries in two ways. First, observe the behavior of those around you, especially peers and managers. When you see them doing or saying things with no ill after-effects, you eventually conclude that that their actions and words are acceptable in this particular company, in a particular situation.

Second, you test boundaries via the consequences of your own behavior. If you make a decision or act in a certain way and there is no immediate negative effect, you conclude that the company condones the decision or action. Indeed, sometimes you might actually be rewarded for certain behaviors and decide that bigger would be even better.

In the process of testing boundaries, you take baby steps toward that invisible line that, if crossed, leads to potential trouble. You might be familiar with the parable of the boiled frog. If you put a frog in a kettle that is filled with cool and pleasant water, and then you *gradually* heat the kettle until it starts boiling, the frog will not notice the incremental changes and be unable to react before it is too late. People are subject to the same experience.

Welcome to the Slippery Slope

Let's examine how the process works. You are a first-time manager and you have developed both a friendly relationship and a business relationship with one of your direct reports. You discuss common interests and share a commitment to family. You frequently talk about things you do outside work and trade stories about raising children.

One day the two of you go to lunch and, in addition to personal talk, spend a good deal of time discussing a work-related issue. Before you were promoted, your boss would expense meals at which you and she discussed business, so you decide it is acceptable to pick up the tab and expense it. You are confident that this is standard practice and your assessment is confirmed when your boss does not question the expense.

You are now just a baby step away from spending only a minor portion of the time on business and deciding to expense the meal. And then, at the end of a long day, with lots more work to do, you expense dinner. Further, you decide you deserve to go to a nice restaurant because you will be working so late. When that is not questioned, you continue to go to the more expensive restaurants for your business lunches. You are sure there is no objection to that practice because no one says anything. And so it goes until you cross that invisible line between accepted business practice and taking undue advantage of your position.

By then, it's often too late to repair the damage. People are usually not admonished about such infractions until they have occurred repeatedly. So by the time it's brought to your attention, it is likely you are already perceived as overstepping your bounds. You can be sure your expenses will be closely scrutinized from then on. Further, it is awkward at the moment you are reprimanded to clarify exactly what the sanctioned expenses are. Any way you phrase the question, it's apt to sound as though you are asking "What exactly *can* I get away with?"

Neither can you console yourself that "no one knows." Even if your boss and boss's boss didn't discuss the situation—which they did—administrative staff usually plays some role in the processing of expenses and they have no reason not to spread the word. Besides, everyone you've taken to these perceived boondoggles sees no reason not to talk about it. You can bet that word has gotten around. By the time you get this kind of information, you are quite likely to be the last one to know.

Certainly this is not to suggest that you ever deliberately set out to misuse and abuse your position. Actually, the fact that you were well intentioned contributed to the visibility of your transgression. When you assume you're not doing anything wrong, you are naturally transparent about it; thus, it becomes common knowledge. In addition, because you are out in the open about your behavior, people might assume that you realize you are out of line and see yourself as so important that you think you can get away with it.

Monitor Yourself

Perhaps you are thinking that you would never make such a mistake as to take advantage of your expense account or other perks. Perhaps not— but that is just that kind of thinking that leaves you vulnerable to making exactly those kinds of mistakes. The problem is that there is a lot of room for interpretation in determining what's allowable in the work world, and there is no clear-cut way to get the "right" answer. Thus, no one is immune to going too far. Over time the corporate environment can slowly and easily seduce you into attitudes and thinking that you would never arrive at in one bold step.

You might witness people at your level and tenure taking long lunches, having alcohol with a meal, or spending more time away from the office on personal business. When this goes on for a while without repercussion, you might assume that, since everyone else is doing it, you can, too. This may or may not be the case. Just because you are not aware of any negative consequences, doesn't mean that there aren't any. It's like keeping up with speeding cars on the highway. It's a mistake to assume that 75 m.p.h. is okay when the speed limit is 65. It only means that no police officer is in the vicinity. If there were one, and you were stopped, "everyone else was doing it, too" would not get you out of a ticket.

Employers sometimes tend to overlook minor infractions because it is easier than confronting them all the time. Overlooking, however, does not mean sanctioning.

In the absence of concrete information, the best rule of thumb is to listen for the inner voice or twinge in your stomach that tells you that you might be crossing an invisible boundary. As you contemplate words or actions, if there is a nagging doubt in the back of your mind, listen to it. What often happens if you don't is that you will not get any feedback that you have crossed a line. This is either because the first time goes unnoticed, or because you have earned an occasional error or two in judgment. Now it becomes easy to assume that whatever you did is permissible.

Ignore These Thoughts!

If you find yourself thinking these thoughts, don't listen to them!

✦ "I don't see why I can't schedule a haircut during work hours. They allow people to take time off work for children's school plays and I don't have any children."

(CONTINUED)

(CONTINUED)

> ✦ "It's no big deal if I'm late for the staff meeting again. No one seems to mind waiting for me and I really need to finish these e-mails now."
>
> ✦ "John leaves two hours early every Friday and no one bothers him. I'm sure I can do the same."

Don't Flaunt It

Due to the fact that there is not a formalized, official policy on certain activities, there is a certain degree of latitude for those who have earned such perks. However, there is also implicit agreement that those privileges are not and cannot be officially and publicly condoned. So even when you are absolutely certain that your actions are within acceptable limits, it is best not to call undue attention to them.

> *Maurice was attending a sales management meeting for a publishing company at an Arizona resort. The meeting was an annual event, but this year the company went way out to reflect a very good year. The meals were lavish and golf, the spa, and so on were on the house. In the evenings, the managers would socialize around the bar, ordering only the finest libations. Celebration and congratulations were the themes of the hour.*
>
> *Maurice mentioned to his boss over one of these after-hour soirees that it would be nice to be able to "live like this with my team back home." Without directly saying so, his boss intimated that a few over-the-top occasions would be tolerated.*
>
> *Upon returning home, Maurice would periodically reward his team with generous outings that would even include their spouses. His boss signed off on the expenses and all was well—that is, until he began talking to his counterparts about it.*

His intention was certainly not to throw it in their faces or cause trouble. The information would be in the context of a conversation about golf, where he would disclose that he took his team to a premier course. Or he would talk about a wonderful wine that he, his team, and their spouses enjoyed at Morton's on Saturday night.

The manager of a top sales team that set company records for five consecutive years throws a party every year after the results are announced. Each year the festivities increase in scope and amount. Her expense reports are never questioned, so she assumes the company appreciates her results enough to absorb the cost of these celebrations.

During a presentation at a management meeting, where she had been asked to share her success secrets, she quipped that she is hesitant to do so lest she has to give up her "extravagant celebrations that keep getting better by the year."

Just because certain things might be accepted, does not mean that they should be advertised. Both Maurice and Mary crossed a line, not because of what they did, but because they called too much attention to it.

To Be a Hero or a Goat

You've reached your position—wherever it might be on the org chart—at least in part because of your willingness to take calculated risks and to be accountable for your decisions. You are certainly expected to continue to do so. In fact, along the way to where you are now you have probably made some miscalculations. Indeed, many companies will tell you that if you never make a mistake, you are not taking enough risks. Thus far, you've learned from past mistakes and been forgiven for them.

In addition, you are now in a place where your value to the company is established. You have a track record for what you have contributed and for the value of your knowledge and expertise. Your very tenure with the company is an asset. Your history with the organization enables you to take what's worked and is working to a new level. Your previous experience keeps you from going down paths that have proven to be dead ends in the past. You can easily be lulled into thinking that there is nothing you could do, if well intentioned and thought out, that will not be forgiven.

Not so. No matter how long you've been with the company, no matter how valuable you are, caution is always important. Of course, this does not mean that you avoid calculated risks or hunker down and always opt for the safe route. That will also get you into trouble. The answer lies in knowing what to risk and when to risk it.

Maureen is a recognized top contributor in R&D of a major pharmaceutical company. She has declined management positions in favor of her love of research. She is among those credited with the development of a widely prescribed drug that is producing profits far beyond what was originally anticipated. Several companies have attempted to recruit her away, with no success due to the compensation, rewards, and recognition her current employer offers.

She is leading a team researching a revolutionary new drug expected to compensate for the revenue loss when the patent on the former drug expires. Maureen is quite vocal and public about her confidence in this project and millions of dollars have been authorized for this research, only to have the drug rejected for FDA approval.

This is a highly visible, widely reported debacle. Along with selected mid- and upper-level managers, Maureen is held responsible, and her reputation throughout the industry takes a drastic dive.

Thomas is the CEO of a global computer company and is convinced that moving from being a product-focused organization to a provider of business solutions will dramatically increase sagging revenues. He is an icon in the industry with a reputation for his innovative, cutting-edge ideas. The parent company is resistant and Thomas draws a hard line in the sand. Soon after, he is asked to step down.

The preceding examples highlight a very important point. No one, for any reason whatsoever, is immune to falling from grace because of what turns out to be a bad decision or a bold stand. In fact, the better the track record—with the accompanying power, authority, and visibility—the greater the possibility of dire consequences.

Check Your Recent Track Record

In the process of assessing whether to take a risk, refer to your track record of late. Are you coming off of a reasonable number of recent wins sufficient enough to buffer a loss? In other words, have you been making mostly deposits in your corporate account? It is more probable that a noticeable flop will be forgiven if you are backed up by some equally noticeable triumphs.

If, on the other hand, you have no recent wins, you are less likely to be forgiven a major miscalculation. And certainly you want to be careful about taking a big risk if you have accumulated a series of losses.

> *CAUTION: Do be careful that a string of recent homeruns doesn't lead you to believe you are invincible and lure you into taking reckless chances that can be interpreted as showing questionable judgment.*

Weigh the Potential Gains Versus Losses

Calculate the advantages if the risk pays off against the negative consequences of failure. Do this for both you and the company. Ask yourself if what you stand to gain is worth what you stand to lose. Consider whether the company can absorb whatever potential loss the action represents.

Check the Visibility Factor

Even if the decision does not represent a huge loss and it comes after a string of wins, be aware of how many people will either witness your success or be privy to a failure. This may or may not be important depending on the particular circumstances, but you should consider it.

Take Ownership of Your Problems

The workplace, like everywhere else, is full of challenges when it comes to dealing with other people. You cannot choose everyone with whom you must interact on a daily basis, and relationships go more smoothly with some folks than they do with others.

Don't Throw Your Weight Around

After you have been around a while and know that you are considered of value, it can be tempting to use your tenure and support to leverage problems or conflicts with others. You might have seen others do it. Perhaps you've even done it yourself and not only were there no negative consequences, but the problem was resolved to your satisfaction. Indeed, it happens all the time.

But that does not mean that it is a good idea to use your power or value to the company to get what you want. You might win a few battles, but with each one, you could be putting yourself closer to losing the war.

> *Samuel had been with a management consulting firm for 10 years and was reputed to be a crackerjack consultant. The company culture was one of cooperation and collaboration among its staff and he was especially skilled at facilitating agreement. Samuel was assigned the leadership of a project for a very big and important client.*
>
> *In the assessment phase, the team uncovered a number of sensitive issues. During the discussions of how to address them, the team resisted Samuel's ideas and he was getting frustrated over his inability to influence and bring the team to consensus. He was certain his approach was the best one and he knew that the buck would stop with him if progress was stalled or the client was in any way dissatisfied.*
>
> *He had access to Marilyn, a high-ranking executive with a huge stake in satisfying this particular client. He sought her input on the situation. When he learned that she shared his perspective, he*

leveraged their conversation and informed the team that Marilyn was aligned with his thinking. This essentially shut down all discussion and they proceeded in the direction Samuel had advocated.

Timely completion of the project was essential. As it moved forward, Samuel frequently used his relationship with Marilyn to expedite progress when there were differences of opinion. He knew the rest of the team did not appreciate this tactic, but he was willing to alienate his colleagues, just this once, if it meant a timely and successful outcome. Unfortunately, he lost the gamble.

Even though the project was a resounding success, Samuel's track record was insufficient to withstand the consequences of running counter to corporate culture. Marilyn did not object to him publicly sharing their conversations, but she found it unacceptable that he used—and thus abused—his relationship with her to ramrod his ideas down his colleagues' throats. Even though he was right on about the issues, his maneuvering simply did not fly.

Samuel could have achieved the same results by inviting Marilyn to participate, in person or via conference call, in the team discussions regarding the particular issues. He should have briefed her prior without attempting to influence her thinking in any direction. If indeed she agreed with him, it would come out during the meeting and the group could react and interact directly with Marilyn. They would have been directly influenced instead of feeling manipulated by Samuel. In addition, if she did not agree, the team would see that she was not being unduly influenced by him. The client would have been well served without Samuel putting himself in jeopardy.

If Marilyn's presence during these debates did not move the process forward and discussions were still bogged down, Marilyn would have seen first-hand what the situation was. She could have then chosen to wield her power or troubleshoot with Samuel how to move the team forward into action. No matter how the process unfolded, Samuel would have managed to operate within acceptable limits.

Think Before Escalating

Before resorting to involving others, explore every possible alternative to resolve your issues. The minute you turn to a higher authority, you are making your problem their problem. Managers are certainly used to this and consider it a part of their job description. However, such action should be a last resort only.

Take a problem higher only when you have entertained and exercised every option to handle it yourself and it is critical to the company—not to you—that it be resolved. When you state the situation, be sure to address how it affects the business or the customer, not how it bothers you.

Maxine provided efficient and effective administrative support and was considered a real asset to the accounting company where she had worked for several years. Upon being reassigned, she was chagrined to find herself dealing with a coworker who consistently failed to pull his share of the load. He was frequently late, and often absent because of doctor appointments and other personal business. Further, he did not follow up on commitments and his work was sloppy.

Maxine was sure that others were aware of the situation and could not understand why nothing was done about it. After tolerating it as long as she could, she tactfully approached her boss about the problem. Maxine was, in effect, told that she needed to learn to manage under the current circumstances.

Well aware that her work was highly regarded, Maxine asked that the she be transferred elsewhere. Soon after, she was assigned to a temporary project off-site. Upon its completion, Maxine was informed that there was no longer a position available for her.

When Maxine was told that the situation would not be addressed, her manager's response should have alerted her to the fact that her coworker's behavior, for whatever reason, was to be tolerated. You cannot always know or guess why certain things are the way they are.

Before Maxine went to her manager, she needed to talk to her coworker herself. If that did not change anything for the better, she should have quietly and tactfully campaigned for another position without making it her manager's problem.

Essentially Maxine was telling her boss "If he stays, I go." It is never a good idea to issue an ultimatum. You could easily be overestimating your importance in any situation, and even if you "win" and get your way, there will surely be some residual resentment.

Go Where You Belong

No matter how prestigious the job or the company is, no matter what the glory or future opportunity is, don't get yourself into a situation that is not a good fit for you. A round peg never gets a square hole to change its shape just to accommodate it.

When you don't fit, it's not a matter of who is right or wrong, what is good or bad, or even about what is best for the company. When your natural style and preferences are not the same as the majority of those around you, it eventually erodes your confidence. Day after day, you experience your work life as if there were something wrong with you, and it's a downward spiral from there. And even if you don't become demoralized, your failure to fit in will be obvious to those you work with and can easily have a negative impact on your reputation in the company.

> *Frank was a star performer as an individual contributor in a chemical research company. He had a top-notch education from a prestigious university and his work was labeled as "brilliant" and "genius." He was elated to be asked to join an elite group working on an unprecedented solution to pollution in rivers and streams. This group was thought to consist of the best and brightest in the company, and to be invited to join was certainly a feather in anyone's cap.*
>
> *As Frank began to integrate himself into the group, he slowly realized that there were significant differences in his work habits and style from those of the others. While Frank worked slowly and*

meticulously, his colleagues had a more driven style. They valued fast while Frank was more comfortable with deliberate. His decision-making involved copious data gathering and analysis to make sure no stone was left unturned. The others were not reckless, but they required far less time to reach their conclusions. The differences were not those of competence or ethics, but rather of style. And the others in the work group viewed Frank's style as cumbersome.

Further, Frank preferred more balance in his life. The group worked up to 16-hour days and came in most weekends. Frank, on the other hand, was an active family man who valued evenings and weekends at home. This put Frank in a real bind. He either had to give up valued personal time and activities or contribute less than his peers. Even when he compromised and came in some weekends, others saw him as the weak link on the team.

Frank was a misfit. Eventually, Frank began to get demoralized and he started to doubt himself. His suggestions were frequently overruled, he was not included in casual conversation, and his opinions were not sought. No one treated him rudely or unprofessionally, but it was clear to Frank that he was not seen as a valued contributor to the team.

Because this team was so visible in the company and held in such high esteem, Frank's plight was common knowledge. Unfortunately, the perception was that he was not such a bright, up-and-coming star as was originally thought.

Know Yourself

The first step to making the right decisions about your work life is to know what constitutes a good fit for you. Prepare a "Best Fit Profile" that includes the following four parts:

* **Paint a realistic picture of your skills, knowledge, abilities, strengths, and weaknesses.** You want every situation to play to

your strengths and benefit from your particular talents. That is not to say that you don't want to seek opportunities to stretch and grow professionally. You do, however, want to make sure that you bring something to the table immediately and that the gap between where you are and where you need to go is not so wide that you can't bridge it.

+ **Identify what you like to do.** You might have skills and abilities that, even though you excel at them, you really do not like to use. No matter how great the opportunity, if it requires you to do a great deal of what you do not enjoy, after a while, enthusiasm wanes and the work could even come to seem like drudgery.

+ **Describe the environment and the circumstances under which you work best.** Even if a job or project is in desperate need of your skills and you love doing the kind of work it requires, if you are in a situation that is out of alignment with your work style preferences, it will take energy to adjust your style to meet that of the workgroup. Depending on how great the differences are, it can be an ever-increasing challenge to adapt. Many assessments can provide you with that kind of information, in addition to your own observations.

+ **Clarify your personal and professional values.** Some examples of personal values are family, travel, health, time with friends, and material possessions. Professional values can include such things as helping others, leadership, influence, acquiring knowledge, and creativity. Make sure that the company or group's values are consistent with your own. If your work environment does not support your values, over time this can become extremely problematic and undermine your satisfaction, if not your success.

You want to compile your profile long before you are faced with a decision so that you can reference it when new opportunities present themselves. If you do not do so, you are liable to be so flattered or blinded by the potential that you say "yes" to a situation that runs counter to your best interests.

This does not mean that you must find a perfect fit. Such situations are rare. After you have itemized your strengths, what you like to do, your work style preference and values, prioritize them. Classify each item as "must have," "prefer to have," or "can live without." Evaluate each new situation and make conscious decisions about what compromises you are willing to make. Be brutally honest with yourself about what you will and will not be able to tolerate.

Action Items

❑ Prepare your Best Fit Profile.

❑ Make a list of your strengths and the skills and abilities that you most enjoy doing.

❑ Identify your personal and professional values.

❑ Assess your work style and preferences, both using formal tools and your own knowledge of the circumstances under which you work best.

❑ Prioritize your values and preferences.

Embrace and Champion Change

In today's world, change is a constant, and you will welcome some changes more than others. The types of change that you are most likely to resist are those that somehow threaten your status or security. If you are an expert and sought-after internal resource on the use of Oracle, you are not likely to welcome a change to Access. If you are a subject-matter expert on a particular product and service, its discontinuation will not come as good news to you.

> *Tom was a highly successful networking systems consultant with a well-respected international firm. His clients raved about him and his peers loved to work on teams with him because they learned so much. When Tom joined the company, the sales and consulting functions*

were separate. However, senior management was moving toward combining them and charging consultants with business development goals.

Tom was quite vocal about his disagreement with this move and he actively lobbied against it. He voiced concerns that "selling" would undermine the integrity of the consulting and that it was a different skill set, one that most consultants did not possess.

When training was offered, Tom attended with such a negative attitude that he failed to achieve any benefit, and he alienated others in the process. He was certain that his consulting prowess would protect him from the need to do anything else. He was right—in the short term.

However, over several years, he fell behind the curve in terms of his value to the company. His peers were increasing their contributions to the top line and new consultants were hired that gladly took on business development responsibilities.

When your company is in the midst of a change that represents some sort of threat or loss, the reflexive reaction is denial. You might tell yourself that "it will never happen," "it won't work," or it "won't affect me." Be an astute observer of your reactions and question yourself relentlessly about the reality of what is going on with you. Make sure that your assessment of the impending or proposed change is accurate, as opposed to a function of your own resistance to it.

Further, even if your resistance is well founded, once a particular change is inevitable, jump on the bandwagon early. Acquire whatever new skills and knowledge the change necessitates. Act as a champion to peers and direct reports by identifying and touting all the reasons why it is a good thing and represents new opportunities for them and for the company. No one, no matter how valued, is immune to the effects and impact of change in the workplace. The key is to welcome and facilitate it instead of opposing and resisting.

> *CAUTION: This does not mean that you have to cheerlead every change that comes down the pike. If you do not see a proposed change as a step in the right direction, and feel that there are real drawbacks, you should not go to extremes to appear otherwise. You will certainly lose credibility if you are perceived as misreading a situation, or worse, untruthful. However, if a change is inevitable, you can still get behind it, do the best you can to make it work, and encourage others to do the same.*

Manage Your Stress Behavior

You feel like you are living in a fishbowl. You are on a steep learning curve. You have more responsibility than ever before. You feel like you are "on" 24/7. For oh-so-many reasons you are stressed, and on some days more so than others. And you're probably dealing with people who are also stressed out.

Most people, when they are stressed, behave in a less-than-constructive and possibly unpleasant manner. Some people will be impatient and short with others. Some become aggressive and demanding. Others withdraw, and still others might become noticeably flustered and ineffectual. No matter what your typical stress behavior, it will not further your cause, and too much of it will eventually undermine you.

You have certainly earned some slack, so on occasion, you can act or react in a way that reflects less-than-your-best self, but you do not want to make it a common occurrence. You are wise to be aware of your stress level at any given moment, so that your actions don't reflect it and chip away at your hard-earned success. Even if you apologize after the fact, there are only so many times that an "I'm sorry" will buy you true forgiveness.

Identify Your Stress Style and Behaviors

Most people have a characteristic way of reacting when they are under stress. Notice exactly how you feel when you are in your stress mode and note what you do and say. Are you like Aunt Pittipat from *Gone With the Wind,* getting all flustered, unable to deal, and needing others to take care of you? Or perhaps you get defensive, grow spines like a porcupine, and fend off others with sharp barbs. Maybe you turn into a schoolyard bully or a rigid drill sergeant. Sometimes it's difficult to pinpoint this by yourself. You might want to seek feedback from a trusted source.

The Story of Eloise, or How I Met My Stressed-Out Self

When I was working with young children, I had to dress up for Halloween. Rather than go as a known character, I put together a costume that represented a caricature. Thus, Eloise was born. She's a sweet thing but she just can't hear the rhythm of life that most other people dance to.

Her hair is peppered with pink sponge curlers and her house-coat is ill-fitting with a stain or two from spilled coffee. She shuffles awkwardly through her days in fuzzy slippers that are matted down and tend to trip her up at times. Eloise's voice is raspy and low, and her speech is slow and thick, as if her tongue were too big and clumsy to find its way easily around her mouth. Poor thing is missing several teeth and her shoulders are rounded and slouched.

However, Eloise tries! She bakes cookies and has the kettle ready to serve tea should anyone drop by to visit. She is a good listener and goes out of her way to make people feel at home. Alas, in spite of her best efforts, she finds herself without much company, and those who do visit don't stay long.

(Note to reader: Be patient. There is a point to all of this.)

Early in my corporate career, I found myself in a meeting with a colleague and two potential customers, and I felt completely intimidated. Having shed my nonprofit feathers, I hadn't yet grown my private-sector skin and I felt totally out of my league. I was certain that I was a fraud and was in terror of being found out.

(CONTINUED)

(CONTINUED)

The harder I tried to look confident and competent, the worse it got—so bad, in fact, that I couldn't even assume a posture. I became increasingly self-conscious: crossing and uncrossing my legs; poising my pen to write and unable to think of a word to put to paper. My discomfort was excruciating, not only to me, but to all who were forced to witness it.

After that meeting, I realized that it was Eloise who had shown up for it. At that instant I knew I had stumbled upon a method to prevent such a fiasco from ever getting in my way again. You see, I totally understood and even liked Eloise. It was just that she couldn't come with me to places where she didn't belong.

Because I no longer needed to resist or stifle her, she lost the power to take over at inopportune moments. This acceptance and nonjudgment provided me with a tool to manage her. When I knew I was walking into a potentially stressful situation, I could consciously leave her behind. I had a handle on her and could even picture her sitting in a comfortable chair and watching TV while I went to work. Even in the very moment when I could feel stress starting to build, I could say in my head "not now, Eloise" and I could manage to put her aside.

This was such a powerful and valuable discovery that I began to share it in my consulting practice, both with individuals and teams. The feedback was consistently positive and clients had fun with the concept and reported they were better able to manage their stressed-out behavior styles.

Once you have identified your style, name it and get to know and understand this part of you intimately. Learn to appreciate this person in the proper setting. You don't need to go so far as develop a persona and costume for your stressed-out self, but if you are so inclined, many have found the exercise useful. If you choose not to create a costume, find a picture that represents your style and learn to recognize it as you are moving into that mode.

Often you can anticipate a stressful situation such as an important presentation, a meeting with a new client, or a problem with a difficult coworker. When you know in advance about such situations, you can prepare yourself mentally and physically so that your behavior is appropriate, professional, and constructive.

Many times, however, you will have no reason to expect to be unusually stressed, but for one reason or another, will find that you are. It is in these situations that you are in danger of pushing boundaries and behaving badly.

Unanticipated stress either appears suddenly or builds slowly and imperceptibly. In either case, by the time it rears its ugly head, the "fight or flight" chemicals are already running rampant through your system. Learn to recognize the signs of stress in your body, and have a plan of action ready for the minute you realize you are going to react from that stress. You may or may not find it helpful to mentally tell your version of Eloise to chill out, so there are other techniques that you can use.

Remove Yourself from the Situation

The best thing to do when you suddenly find yourself stressed beyond your ability to control it is to find a reason to delay the interaction until you have a chance to recover, think the situation through, and deal with it calmly and constructively.

If appropriate, you can say something like "I don't think this is the best time to have this discussion. Let's meet first thing tomorrow morning." Or you can offer "I cannot give this matter my full attention now since I am dealing with a deadline. I think this is important so let me get back to you when I can give it the focus it deserves."

If such comments do not fit the circumstances, or for some reason are inappropriate, make any excuse that will buy you time. "I have a meeting," or "I promised to call John by 9," will allow you time to decompress.

Take a Small Break

At times there is no escape. You will be in a meeting with peers and management, or with an important client. You will be addressing an issue that needs immediate resolution. Although you cannot totally remove yourself, you can excuse yourself for a moment to go to the restroom. Use that respite to take some deep breaths, shut your eyes, and calm yourself as best you can. Some people have found that visualizing a peaceful, special place puts them in a better frame of mind to deal constructively. If you meditate, even a few minutes can have a calming effect.

Speak Slowly and Softly

When you are dealing under stress, your own behavior can cue your body to relax. Therefore, deliberately lower your voice and speak slowly and deliberately. Choose your words carefully and if you feel angry statements forming, close your mouth and *do not speak at all*. It is probably no secret to anyone involved that you are stressed and quite likely they are also. So there is no need to go to great lengths to camouflage your state. What is important is that you do not do or say anything you will come to regret. So if you cannot trust what is going to come out of your mouth, be quiet.

Virtual Alert

If you are on the phone, either one-on-one or a conference call, being silent can lead the other(s) to wonder whether you are still there. Simply announce to them "I'm still here; I'm just thinking."

Don't Seek Out the Opportunity to Express or Act from Your Stress

Often the source of stress is another's behavior and you discover it when he or she is not present. You get an e-mail that someone is not going to meet an important deadline. Your boss calls you to gripe about a decision made by one of your direct reports. You receive a spreadsheet that is inaccurate and totally unacceptable.

Oh how tempting to contact the responsible party and let them have it. You can imagine how delicious it would feel to let them know, in no uncertain terms, your reaction to what they did or did not do.

Nine times out of ten, the momentary pleasure will not compensate for the consequences of your unprofessional, perhaps inappropriate behavior. Don't gamble. Wait until you are calm and can deal with the issue in a rational and professional manner.

Don't Let Things Build Up

Do not, however, let things go. Sometimes, once you calm down, the idea of a confrontation can be uncomfortable and unpleasant. You might want to convince yourself that "it's no big deal."

Usually, though, it is a big deal, and it will happen again. If you wait until you reach your limit to deal with it, your reaction is sure to be disproportionate to the one incident that set it off. The person on the receiving end, to this point, had no clue what was going on with you, and he or she will be taken aback by your behavior. Indeed, it will look like an overreaction, no matter what the issue is.

CAUTION: This does not mean that you have to address everything that you might find a nuisance or the slightest bit annoying. You have to know what to swing at and what to tolerate. Everyone can have habits or idiosyncrasies that wear on your nerves. Learn to truly tolerate and overlook as much as you can. Let the needs of your job responsibilities and the best interests of the business guide you in determining what to address and what to let go of.

There Is No Downtime

You will often find yourself in work-related social situations where everyone is relaxed and in play mode. These occasions might feel exactly like a night out with friends or family. They are not.

You are always "on" when you are with colleagues or customers. Therefore, you are always in jeopardy of making a mistake from which you will be unable to recover. In fact, you are in even greater danger in social situations because it is easier to let down your guard and reveal information or behave in a manner you wouldn't even consider in a work environment.

Be careful about alcohol consumption, which further erodes your inhibitions. Even if others are ordering drinks left and right, know your own limits and don't let yourself get beyond a point where you are in control.

This cautionary advice also applies when you are out only with friends and family, if you might be in a place where colleagues and customers are present. Although it might not cost you your job or reputation, you don't want your manager to see you in the grocery store in the midst of a heated argument with your spouse. Your cause will not be furthered if a customer witnesses you lose your temper with your toddler.

> *Eileen was a contractor for small field office of an engineering company. She had consistently exceeded expectations and received rave reviews from clients. She was hoping to be offered a full-time position. Her invitation to the Christmas party was a sure sign she was being considered as a permanent member of the team.*
>
> *Eileen had been dating a man for a short time and invited him to be her escort. Unfortunately, he got quite drunk at the dinner and was boisterous and offensive, making everyone uncomfortable. The office manager concluded that Eileen's decision to bring this man to the party reflected poor professional judgment. Not only was she not considered for a full-time position, but she was no longer offered primo contract opportunities for fear that she would demonstrate similar faulty judgment in front of a valued client.*

Reality Check: How Are You Doing?

Use the following questions to help you ensure that you avoid the hidden traps and potential pitfalls that come with success in your company.

+ Who in my department and in the company might be observing my behavior? Why?

+ What expectations might I be setting in terms of work and relationships with colleagues? Will I be able to maintain them over time? If not, what can I do now to back it up a bit?

+ What perks and privileges have I earned? What are the acceptable limits? How do I know? How can I find out?

+ What perks and practices are sanctioned but not "advertised?"

+ What work-related risks am I contemplating? What are the potential gains versus the potential losses? Can I withstand a loss? What is my recent track record? How visible is this to the company?

+ Do I have any challenges or issues with coworkers? What is the best plan of action to address these issues?

+ Do I have any situations in the near future that I can anticipate will be stressful? What can I do to prepare ahead of time?

+ What is my style when I am stressed? What can I practice in the moment to mitigate it?

If you are contemplating a change in work—such as a new department or a new job—ask yourself the following questions:

+ What are my values?

+ What are my work style and preferences? How do I like to be managed? How do I like to interact with my colleagues?

+ Is this new situation consistent with my values and preferences?

BLOW YOUR HORN SOFTLY

You Are Only as Great as Other People Say You Are

With turnover, power shifts, and the mere size and complexity of contemporary organizations, you cannot be certain that others will notice your value and achievements without your deliberately calling attention to them. If you want to progress in your career, get promoted, and take on expanded responsibilities, you need a strategy to do so. An integral component of that strategy is to ensure that your good work gets recognized by those who can help you move ahead. This includes not only those who can directly influence your progress, but also colleagues who might have these people's ear. Your goal is to build a stellar reputation at all levels of your organization and in the broader professional community.

You want to create a perception of yourself as strong in the skills and abilities needed to move you toward your career goals. It is a distinct advantage if you are reputed to be competent, committed, and professional. You want your name to come up when special task forces are formed and when important projects are being assigned.

Be Careful Not to Turn People Off

However, you must be careful not to mistake singing your own praises as music to anyone else's ears. Although it is essential that you advertise your strengths and contributions, you must accomplish it in a subtle, almost imperceptible fashion. Your efforts to further your own career and reap the rewards of your hard work can easily backfire. If you go about self-promotion like a loose cannon, you can end up shooting yourself in the foot. You must avoid appearing too full of yourself, overambitious, and a poor team player. You don't want to be seen as arrogant or a shameless self-promoter. You must be careful not to antagonize others lest they come to resent you to the point that they would enjoy—if not set up—a situation where you fall flat on your face.

> *Stanley was getting his MBA and concurrently working for a large hardware store chain. He observed that the people who were doing well in the organization were consistently and deliberately bringing their work to the attention of others. Stanley was hired upon graduation, and from very early he began to call attention to his strengths. He quickly learned who could help him progress and was also diligent in building relationships with everyone throughout the company. Stanley was considered a high-potential employee and was often selected for special assignments. He was offered every chance for professional development, which gave him many opportunities to blow his horn in front of more people. In addition, Stanley joined several outside associations and networking groups and took advantage of every opportunity to tout his professional prowess.*

> *Eventually, and quite deliberately, he built a reputation as a superior strategic thinker. Stanley was a bright, articulate young man with a charismatic and commanding presence. When he was recruited away by a competitor, he naturally set about the same self-campaigning that had worked so well for him at his preceding company. Somewhere along the way, however, his rapid movement slowed to a crawl. Stanley began a stealth job search and successfully transitioned to another hardware chain; but again, his progress never regained its early momentum.*

Stanley was rewarded for his initial horn-blowing with attention, praise, and rapid progress in the company. Unfortunately, his reputation as an excellent performer eventually turned into one of an incessant braggart. His constant efforts to call attention to himself began to irritate people and he was noticed more for his self-promotional efforts than for the quality of his work, even though the latter continued to be of a very high caliber.

The strategy behind establishing a reputation for excellence is to get other people to sing your praises. You can make this happen by the manner in which you go about promoting your skills and accomplishments. The secret is to circulate positive information about yourself without calling inordinate attention to the fact that you are doing so. You want to camouflage your self-promotion as casual conversation, a search for information, problem solving, or support for others.

Rely on Facts, Not Editorials

The best way to go about letting others know what you can do is to seek and create opportunities to tell people about what you have actually accomplished in the recent past. You offer a great deal of information about yourself via concrete examples that describe what you have done and specifically how you have contributed. The key is to talk about yourself in such a way that others can draw their own conclusions from objective data, instead of you offering "editorial" comments about how good you are. A comment such as "I am an extremely organized person" won't resonate as well as an example of when you managed several complex projects at one time.

There are two behind-the-scenes steps to effective self-promotion. The first is to identify what you have done and what it says about you. The second is to know where you want to go. When the opportunity arises, you want to tell people stories that convey specifically what you have done in the past. These are accounts of your prior accomplishments and they showcase your value. To do this succinctly while hitting all the important points, you must be ready. This means that you prepare this information in advance, so that you are prepared to speak about it at a moment's notice.

Identify What You Have Done

Create a file that contains a chronicle of your accomplishments covering the past three or so years. Also, keep any appreciative e-mails and notes from colleagues and customers. Once you have collected your stories to date, get in the habit of adding to the file on an ongoing basis in order to keep it current.

You might already know of the need to capture and articulate your accomplishments when you are looking for a new job and preparing your resume. Actually, this is an important activity throughout your career, regardless of your current employment situation. Sometimes it's hard to get started; however, in a world where you must constantly communicate your worth, this practice is absolutely essential to your career success.

Following is a list of questions to help guide your thinking:

✦ Have you made money for the company?

✦ Have you increased sales?

✦ Have you offered ideas and suggestions that made the company more competitive?

✦ Have you saved money?

✦ Have you gone out of your way to please an internal or external customer?

✦ Have you negotiated with vendors to save the company money?

✦ Have you streamlined processes to make them more efficient?

✦ Have you come up with ideas to save time on routine tasks?

✦ Have you reduced costs?

✦ Have you led or participated in any special projects?

✦ Are you especially proficient on particular computer programs?

- ✦ What other languages do you know?

- ✦ Have you won any awards?

- ✦ Have you earned any certificates?

The above is only a partial list of the kinds of accomplishments that you might have to your credit. You can also make a list of the traits, characteristics, or abilities that you possess. You might be a good problem solver, a creative thinker, or a good communicator, among many other things. Once you create such a list, identify what you have done that exemplifies these traits, characteristics, or abilities. In other words, think of specific times when you have been organized, creative, and so on. These will constitute your stories.

> *CAUTION: Don't edit or judge your accomplishments. Capture all of them without discarding any of them because you decide it's not a big deal or that you were just doing your job. You never know when a particular achievement will be relevant under a particular set of circumstances. What seems like an unremarkable solution can take on enormous importance when a similar problem arises.*

What, How, and So What?

Once you have a list of your accomplishments, chronicle all the relevant details. Each story should tell *what* the reason was that you did what you did, *how* you went about doing it, and the *so what:* how it was beneficial to the company.

- ✦ **What:** The *what* of your story describes the problem, situation, need, or opportunity that prompted some action on your part. You either identified the issue on your own or perhaps you were asked to address it. You might have taken over the management of an administrative team that was not operating at maximum efficiency. Perhaps as a floor supervisor for a food manufacturer, you were concerned with less-than-satisfactory adherence to safety standards and a poor safety record. Maybe as a key staff member of a non-profit organization, you were tasked with securing grant money to improve neighborhood schools. If you are an office assistant, you might have noticed that the processing of expense reports was slow and cumbersome.

✦ **How:** The *how* details exactly what actions you took to address the *what*. Include all the steps, and speak to the challenges and road-blocks that you encountered along the way.

✦ **So what?** Finally you want to identify the *so what*. How did your actions benefit the company, department, or customer? This under-scores your ability to identify, focus, and contribute based the needs of the business.

You might not be able to immediately bring to mind the *what, how,* and *so what* because you are not in the habit of paying attention to them. You usually see something that needs doing and just do it in the course of your day. You might not consider it remarkable—just a matter of doing your job. You might not think about the reasons behind it or how it ben-efits the business. However, there usually is a reason to tackle something and it is important to know what it is.

A story should always include the business need that motivated your actions and a statement of the beneficial results. Including this informa-tion when you tell your stories says two important things about you. The first is that you are alert to opportunities to add value. Second, it shows that you prioritize your decisions and actions according to what is best for the business. In today's world, there is no value placed on doing something just because it seems like a good idea.

Story Examples

The following examples demonstrate how to organize and complete your stories. I will talk later about when and how to weave them easily into a conversation and make the fact that you are blowing your own horn barely noticeable.

The Sales Manager:

When I took over the Western region, sales were down and there was a clear expectation for me to increase revenues. I didn't want to come in like gangbusters and just start changing everything, so I held a two-day off-site meeting within the first few weeks of my taking the job. The agenda was focused more on my listening than talking, and included social time in the evenings. I announced that I would be meeting with each representative individually to get a handle on best practices and support their success.

During these one-on-one sessions, my original suspicion was confirmed that the reps were focused only on selling products and paying no attention to strategically building and maintaining relationships. Thus, customers were easy prey for other vendors with a one-time better deal.

I shared this observation with all the reps via a conference call and introduced the value of a relationship-management program to gain ongoing customer loyalty. To gain buy-in, I selected well-respected reps to help structure and implement the initiative. I then had them champion the idea to their colleagues. As a result, we built a pool of loyal customers and in the last three years sales have increased by close to 40 percent.

The Administrative Assistant:

I noticed that our office operating expenses seemed awfully high. On my own initiative, I took a hard look at where the money was going. I found that we were ordering office supplies from several different vendors and our routine service and maintenance expenses were excessive.

I talked with several suppliers in order to select one that would offer the best pricing and service. I was able to negotiate discount rates on high-volume items such as paper, file folders, toner cartridges, and the like. This not only saved money, but it greatly simplified inventory tracking and payment processing. From nurturing and building a strong relationship with the company rep, we get outstanding service on rush orders and returns, in addition to substantial discounts on large orders such as furniture and cubicle structures.

I also taught myself to do the routine maintenance and service on our office equipment such as the copier, fax, and printers. We were able to significantly reduce those expenses as well.

The Human Resources Generalist:

We were experiencing supervisor turnover far above the industry average and exit interviews were of no help in uncovering why. I started talking to people casually and off the record about what the problem might be. I learned that the supervisors felt they lacked the necessary skills to do their jobs and did not receive the support they needed from the managers above them. Our current training offerings focused heavily on technical and safety programs with no formal development on how to manage people. Senior management had historically been reticent about such offerings.

My next step was to make a case for supervisor and manager training without betraying confidentiality. I enlisted the support of my boss to get senior management to approve a company-wide assessment of training needs, knowing that it would document the problem. Consequently, I prepared a report for senior management highlighting the results and emphasizing the cost of continually replacing supervisors.

As a result, we developed ongoing formal programs and coaching for supervisors and their managers. Performance reviews of both supervisors and managers were expanded to include items that measured management skills. It's been a gradual culture change. Over the past several years, supervisor retention has improved by 50 percent.

Action Items

❏ Make a list of your accomplishments and contributions over the past three years. Include as many as you have without leaving out any because you might judge them as unimportant.

❏ Turn each accomplishment into a story that tells what you did and how you did it, and includes the beneficial business result.

What Do Your Stories Say About You?

Whereas your stories contain important information about what you have achieved, they also speak to your work ethic, your traits, and your abilities and skills. Your stories are a mirror that reflects you at your best; they highlight your strengths, illustrate your best points, and allow others to "discover" what you want them to know about you.

Therefore, the next step after you have completed your stories is to identify what they say about you. Let's examine each of the preceding examples to illustrate this process.

The sales manager is a person who possesses the following:

+ Leadership and management skills

+ Strategic sales expertise

+ Knowledge of how to get buy in and cooperation

+ Coaching skills

+ Analytical skills

+ Relationship-building skills

- Interviewing skills
- Communication skills

The administrative assistant is a person who demonstrates the following:

- Initiative
- An appreciation and investment in the needs of the business
- Negotiation skills
- Relationship-building skills
- Office-management skills
- Inventory-tracking skills
- Routine maintenance and repair skills
- Cost-saving abilities

The human resource manager possesses the following:

- Political savvy
- Interviewing skills
- The ability to earn trust and keep confidences
- Communication skills
- Presentation skills
- The ability to influence without authority
- An understanding of organizational dynamics and processes

As you identify what each of your stories conveys about you, you will start to notice redundancies. These constitute your strongest skills, traits, abilities, and characteristics. They sum up what is most valuable about you.

Action Items

❑ For each story, identify what it conveys about your skills, talents, knowledge, and characteristics.

❑ Identify those that come up over and over and note them as your strengths.

Know Where You Are Going

After you have completed your stories and identified the strengths that they represent, the next step is to identify what about yourself you want to advertise. You want to call attention to those strengths, talents, and experiences that are aligned with your goals. You need to be clear about what they are so that you can offer only the data that recommends you for what you want to do.

It does you absolutely no good to talk about everything and anything. There is no point to random ramblings about "I've done this" and "I can do that" if they don't advance you toward your career objectives. There is no reason to let people know that you are a standout manager if you prefer the role of an individual contributor. It does not further your career to tout your nursing bedside manner if you want to be an administrator.

As you formulate your short- and long-term goals, be sure to take into account how your growth in that particular direction aligns with your company's goals and objectives. You want to demonstrate that you are thinking not just of what you need and want, but what is good for the company's future as well. You might not always be able to emphasize that you have taken this into consideration, but there will be occasions when it is appropriate to mention.

Action Items

❒ Identify what you want to be doing in the next three to five years. Note the next steps toward those goals.

❒ Examine your strengths and note those that recommend you toward your next steps and ultimate goal. Identify the stories that speak most directly to those strengths.

Ignore These Thoughts!

If you find these thoughts running through your mind, don't listen to them!

✦ "I don't have to put myself to all this trouble. I will know exactly what to say when the time comes to say it."

✦ "I'm not going to worry about this story. It really isn't all that important."

✦ "I'm just not that comfortable talking about myself. People will know what I can do."

Identify and Create Opportunities to Tell Your Stories

Once you have an acute awareness of your strengths and ample supply of stories and examples that document them, you certainly want to share this kind of information at every opportunity. The first rule, however, is to make sure that the parties who are hearing your stories actually *want* to listen to them. You want those you are talking with to be interested, for one reason or another, in what you have to say.

I said earlier that the best self-promotion doesn't look like self-promotion at all. Rather, it is in some way relevant to a particular situation or conversation and, in some fashion, adds value.

Julie had been recently promoted from a supervisor to a management position and was attending her first regional meeting. She was asked to introduce herself and tell a little about her background. She had come prepared. She offered some facts about her background and included several stories in her introduction. Julie saw this meeting as a chance to blow her horn and took every opportunity to talk about what she had accomplished during her tenure with the company.

As the meeting continued over several days, her peers had heard quite enough. They actually started to avoid her whenever possible and each returned to their local offices with not-very-complimentary stories about the new manager from Detroit.

Make It Relevant

When you tell your stories they should weave naturally into the flow of the conversation. You want to offer information at a time when others are interested and attentive, perhaps even appreciative. Certainly, you don't want them to notice that you are sharing these stories, even partially, to promote yourself. Actually, if that is the *only* reason you are offering up the information, you probably don't want to do so.

Let's take the example of the sales manager. He is at a company-wide meeting, and over lunch, his peers are discussing the challenges of getting reps to be more strategic and disciplined in tracking and planning their sales activities. He offers this:

Boy, do I ever understand! I know how hard it is to get people to do things differently, especially when it involves a lot of documentation and preplanning. I was brand new to my region when I had to increase sales and motivate my reps to follow a relationship-management strategy.

The sales manager can pause here. Certainly he has piqued his colleagues' curiosity enough to invite a question about what he did. In response to this inquiry, he can continue like this:

I really struggled with how I was going to influence them to take on the additional work and research required to make the strategy successful. I was afraid they would only go through the motions. After some sleepless nights, I finally came up with the idea to include some key reps on a task force to work out the details and put the strategy in place. I figured I would be able to count on them to influence their peers to actually use the system. It took a little longer, but it worked and our sales went up by 40 percent. I'm not usually a patient man, so it took some discipline to sit through those calls. In the end, though, it was worth it.

Notice that his story was a direct response to the topic under discussion and how he offered it to perhaps spark some ideas on how his peers might address the issue. There are numerous other topics of discussion that would give the sales manager an opportunity to recount his story: increasing sales, changing things when brand new to a job, getting buy-in for changes, customer loyalty, and planning and leading off-site meetings.

CAUTION: The only appropriate time to offer self-promoting information is when it is in the interests of the other party and that interest is genuine. It is of critical importance that you not misinterpret the suggestions in this chapter to mean that you should engineer an opportunity to appear to be doing one thing when it is really just an excuse to blow your horn. Helping others and self-promotion is not an oxymoron. You can do both at the same time and should always make supporting another a priority over calling attention to yourself.

The administrative assistant can bring his cost-cutting efforts to his boss's attention by bringing them up when appropriate. For instance, he can send her an e-mail apprising her that he has negotiated discount pricing with a particular vendor and, if she has no objections, he will be using them exclusively in the future. Certainly, his manager would want to stay informed.

When reviewing the budget for the annual holiday party, he can mention how much he has saved by doing routine maintenance and service, and suggest that they might enhance the budget for the party a bit. He can let his colleagues in other departments know about the office-supply vendor in case they want to do the same. He can also offer to help them with their equipment maintenance.

The human resource manager can recount her story during several different kinds of conversations: making a case to senior management; reducing turnover; conducting employee assessments; and manager development.

Tell Personal Stories

You do not have to limit your stories to professional accomplishments in order to communicate your strengths. Examples from your personal life will serve the same purpose. If you are highly organized, an account of how you managed a project for your daughter's scout troop or your son's field trip will communicate that information. If you know how to make things happen, you can tell how you petitioned the city to rezone property adjacent to your home. You can demonstrate leadership through a story of how you initiated an annual block party in your neighborhood. Just as with professional accomplishments, these stories should be relevant to the subject at hand.

Being ready to tell personal stories provides you with additional opportunities to blow your horn. They add to the number of topics that might be relevant and of interest to others. Remember, you will build your reputation over time, so you want as many examples of your strengths and value as you can possibly have.

Seek Input from Others

One way to call attention to what you know and what you're doing is by seeking input from others. The human resource manager in the preceding example could call attention to herself *before* she even began her project. She could contact colleagues inside and outside the company to get their input on the best way to go about conducting the training needs assessments. She could ask them about their past experiences and ask for any advice on avoiding unintended consequences.

Such conversations would provide her with ample opportunity to demonstrate the depth of her knowledge about the subject and her understanding of organizational dynamics. Most likely, those she talks with will invite her to keep them posted, making her *actually obligated* to let them know of her results.

You can approach others for support for all kinds of reasons. They might have experience on a project similar to one that has just been assigned to you. They might have gotten an opportunity you want to vie for in the future and you can inquire as to how they went about achieving it. They might have used a software program you are thinking about trying. People are always a rich source information. During these conversations, there should be a natural opportunity for you to talk about what you have done and about what you already know.

This means that you need to keep current on who is doing what in your organization. I have talked a great deal about the importance of building relationships and this is another good reason to do so. Sometimes you can find out what people are doing from your company intranet or newsletter. Often you have to rely on relationships to provide you with this kind of information.

> CAUTION: *Be sure that your requests for information and advice are genuine and not manufactured to provide you with a platform to promote yourself. Someone is sure to know if you are making up a reason to contact them, and it is bound to have a negative impact on the way he or she perceives you.*

Before requesting information or help from someone else, you should gather as much data as you can through your own reconnaissance efforts. Make sure that you really need the information you are seeking and that you have no other options to obtain it. As stated before, although this gesture is a good way to camouflage blowing your horn, you do not want to be disingenuous in creating such opportunities.

Offer Support to Others

Again, by staying informed about what is going on in the company, you can discover opportunities to showcase your talents by offering to help others in situations where you have experience and expertise. You need to be careful, however, that the manner in which you offer this support is not misinterpreted to mean that you lack confidence in someone else's ability to rise to the occasion.

If you know of someone who is about to undertake a project or tackle a problem with which you have had past experience, begin by letting her or him know that you have been in a similar situation. Give a short overview of your story, and be sure to *be brief.*

Ask a lot of questions instead of besieging the other person with the details of your circumstance. Your goal here is to gain the opportunity to participate in some way that shows, rather than tells, what you can do. If this is the first time you've spoken to this individual, learn about his or her background. Ask how he or she came to get this particular assignment and what he or she anticipates the slam dunks and the challenges to be. If you have not previously done so, the objective of this first contact is to establish yourself as a credible resource, and the best way to do this is by doing more listening than talking.

Do not come out and say, "I can help you." This leaves it open for the person to respond with a polite "No, thank you" or "I will let you know," and you might never hear from him or her again. If you ask questions that give you the opportunity to share more about your experience in the course of a conversation, you are demonstrating, rather than espousing, your value. Be careful not to be preachy or sound like you have all the answers. Make sure the conversation is a genuine exchange.

As the encounter concludes, state that you enjoyed talking with him or her. By this time you should have gathered enough information to offer specific support, such as sending the person a document or referring him or her to a Web site. Suggest that you will follow up at a later date. Keep the ball in your court, but do not be pushy. Let the other person direct how and how often you will have input. Also, be willing to make this conversation the last one. You have already gained something by making the other person aware of your story, so if this is the end of it, so be it.

You can create many opportunities to demonstrate your talents, so don't get invested in any one particular situation to the point that you become annoying and perceived as in the way.

> *NOTE: You build your reputation over time, with numerous opportuni-ties to show and tell what you can do. Do not get too attached to any one opportunity, forum, or person. Be patient and trust that word will get out. It is more important to let a particular situa-tion go by than to work so hard to get your story in that it becomes obvious that you are about self-promotion.*

Get Others to Talk About Themselves

Another way to create the chance to blow your horn is to get another person talking about him- or herself and the things this person has done. You can invite him or her to do so with questions such as this: "I under-stand you had a great meeting in Atlanta. How did you pull that off given the way sales are going?"

During the course of such a conversation, there will probably be chances for you to offer up some of your own experiences. Be sure that they fit naturally into the flow and that you do not then dominate the conver-sation. I cannot overemphasize that you must be genuinely interested in the other person, not just motivated by the desire to create an opportu-nity to talk about yourself.

Tell Your Stories Naturally

When you are telling your stories, you don't want to sound like you are reciting. Although you want to state facts, you want to do so in a con-versational tone, relating the experience from your personal point of view as you would when telling about any other event in your life. Share your reactions, as well as talk about what you did, so that the listener can relate to you.

Following are some examples of how to do so:

I was really worried about the negative attitude of the call-center staff and how it was transparent to the customers. My boss was on me to do something to turn around my direct reports, and I wasn't sure where to start. I was a first-time supervisor and really didn't know a lot about motivating people. I did some reading and talked to some of my friends about what I might do.

I began to pay attention and reward people for the things they were doing right. I held meetings to specifically address customer service and offered periodic perks for reducing customer wait time and increasing satisfaction. I did things like bring in bagels and cream cheese when our survey results improved, and I posted our numbers weekly. My boss actually congratulated me during a staff meeting and asked me to share with the others how I did it. It really felt good to have turned things around and to be recognized for it.

I sometimes get impatient with people who take no initiative to figure anything out for themselves. I had this demanding internal customer who came to me every time he had the slightest problem with the system. He would fuss and fume, and I found myself getting more and more annoyed and testy. It got so bad that when I saw his name come up on my phone, I was tempted to let it go to voice mail. Then one day I gave myself a good talking to and decided to check my attitude at the door and go out of my way to help this guy. I offered to sit with him and walk him through the fundamentals. I discovered that he really wanted to learn but wasn't comfortable finding his way around the new system. He was embarrassed about calling attention to his remedial skills and relieved that I volunteered to help remedy his situation without judging him for it. Well, I made a fast friend after that. He was so appreciative, he even e-mailed my boss and my boss's boss about what I did. It was sure a valuable lesson to me about customer service.

I'd been campaigning for months to get a chance to learn Access and my boss finally agreed to send me to classes. Well when I got there, I was in no way prepared for how complex the software was and I was afraid I'd bitten off more than I could chew. I knew the expectations would be high when I came back from the training. I can't tell you how many late nights I put in so I wouldn't embarrass myself by showing up as less than proficient. Well, it really paid off. I've come to be known as the "Access Guru" in the office.

Notice how the personal comments tend to soften the stories. The accomplishments still come across, but by sharing the personal side, it doesn't sound like bragging. Rather, the individual is simply sharing an experience.

> *CAUTION: You want to be somewhat self-effacing when you tell your stories using such phrases as "I was fortunate to...," or "I was a little worried about...." However, don't go overboard with your humility. You don't want to risk being perceived as insincere or lacking in self-confidence.*

Give Credit to Others

Talking about others is an excellent way to go about self-promotion. When you are telling a story, you can do so in terms of how someone else helped, mentored you, or contributed. Your accomplishment will still come across even though you are not shining the spotlight solely on yourself.

I didn't have a clue as to how I was going to get the management team to turn in their expense reports in a timely fashion. My boss was on me to do something about it and I certainly didn't have the authority to mandate that these people meet our accounting deadlines. I don't know what I would have done if Terry hadn't offered to help. He sat with me and coached me through my options, pointing out the strengths and possible pitfalls of each one. He really helped me sort out my thinking and guided me in the right direction.

With his sage counsel, I reviewed our processes and realized how cumbersome they were and got my boss's permission to streamline them. When expense reports started to show up in a more timely fashion, I took it as an opportunity to thank the managers and explain how helpful this was to accounting. The situation is much improved and my boss is quite pleased with me and my results.

Talk About Mistakes

Another way to showcase your abilities is to talk about mistakes you have made and what you learned from them. This is another opportunity to blow your own horn without blatantly calling attention to the fact that you are doing so.

Boy, was my face ever red. I was brand new to the logistics depart-ment and I developed a plan whereby we could offer next-day furni-ture delivery. I proudly broached the idea at a staff meeting and it was politely pointed out that we are competing in a low-cost segment of the market and our margins couldn't bear the cost. I learned the hard way that the logistics strategy needed to support the business needs. I am pleased to report that since then I have managed to earn a track record of creating logistic strategies that take into account all relevant variables: maximizing profitability, meeting customer expec-tations, and maintaining our competitive edge in the marketplace.

I was really excited to get the concierge job. I love working with and pleasing people and I went out of my way to get to know the guests and make sure their stay at the hotel was a good one. After I had fig-ured out how to get much-in-demand theatre tickets for a guest, a desk clerk called me "Miss Perky," and it was not intended as a com-pliment. I worried that my enthusiasm was seen as phony or unwel-come and thought I'd better tone it down a notch. You can imagine my surprise when my boss called me into his office and asked if I was unhappy with the job. He suggested that my attitude and customer service skills had noticeably fallen from what they used to be.

Well that was a real wake-up call and from then on I learned to validate my reactions to casual comments before taking them too seriously. I went right back to my natural way of doing my job and have been commended often for providing responsive and superior guest services.

Enroll Others

There are some relationships with colleagues, your boss, and internal and external customers in which it is perfectly appropriate to enroll their support in spreading the word about you and what you have contributed. These people are those with whom you have a solid relationship that has been built over time. You must use good judgment in determining who to ask for this kind of support. You want them to know and trust you enough so that they do not feel used or exploited in any manner. In order words, you want to be sure you have a lot of money in your bank account with these people.

Sample Situations

When that is the case, it is appropriate to share your career goals and ask for their participation. The time to do this is in those moments when your accomplishments are in some way a topic of conversation, as in the following situations:

- ✦ **A customer thanks you for going out of your way to solve a difficult issue.** "As always, it was my pleasure. If you are comfortable, I would appreciate your making [my manager] aware that I did this. It could make a difference in my getting the promotion."

- ✦ **Your boss commends you for a job well done.** "Thanks. I am proud of my results and appreciate all your support in the process.

Would you mind letting [your boss] know about the role I played?"

+ **A colleague comments on your excellent technical skills.**
"Thank you. I am grateful for my gifts in this area. You could really help me out by bringing this to the attention of [your manager]. I would love to be a part of the project team he's putting together."

Note in the preceding examples that it's okay to state your pride in your accomplishments and talents. Indeed, to do so makes others comfortable. False modesty is usually noticeable as such, and you appear less than genuine. Owning how you feel about what you do will lead others to trust in your sincerity. It also gives them permission to do the same with you.

Support Others

Another good way to enlist the support of others is for you to help them by calling attention to their strengths and accomplishments. Be alert to every opportunity to bring colleagues to the attention of their constituency, customers, and management. Send them e-mails of appreciation with copies to their boss. Ask them whether you can show their work to others or tell another how they successfully handled a difficult situation. Talk about their achievements at meetings, over lunch, and in other public forums. Ask them to share their experiences and accomplishments with an invitation such as "Brittany, tell the group about the customer you had the other day." This will make them want to do the same for you.

CAUTION: This does not mean that you want to "keep score." Nor do you cease your efforts if others do not return the favor in kind. Also, do not offer insincere or unwarranted public praise. Everything you do must be genuine, offered in good faith, and a gesture for its own sake. You must trust that "what goes around comes around," and not resort to an Excel spreadsheet to track the results of your goodwill.

Everything Says Something About You

Everything you say or do communicates something about the kind of person you are. You can blow your horn not only with your accomplishments, but by the way you tell your stories. They can speak not only to what you've done and what your strengths are; they can also provide information about your attitudes and personal characteristics.

Let's look at two different managers talking about having to provide sensitive feedback to a direct report. They both begin their story by relating this:

"Sally was a good worker, but she could sometimes be so abrasive that others did not want to work with her. I had to give her feedback about this and was able to get the message across so that her behavior noticeably improved after I spoke with her."

That's where the similarity ends.

Jonathan adds, "I knew Sally meant well and would be surprised by this feedback. She makes a valuable contribution but was undermining her effectiveness with her abruptness. She had been short with me on occasion, so I used those times as the examples I needed to help her understand the effect she had on people. I wanted to give her the tough message as gently as possible, but directly enough so that she could hear and act on it."

On the other hand, Polly continues:

"I was all too pleased to give Sally this feedback after being on the receiving end of her wrath several times."

By Jonathan's words, you can conclude that he is a sensitive, supportive manager who wants to bring out the best in his people. Not so with Polly. She sounds like she personalizes the behavior of her direct reports and it's possible that she actually takes pleasure in somehow retaliating.

Be alert that you are *always* "saying" something about yourself, not only with your words but with your actions as well. This means that you do not have to rely solely on your stories in order to circulate information about who you are and what you can do. If you talk about how you shoveled snow for a neighbor or went out of your way to find the owners of a hurt dog, you are "telling" people that you are kind and thoughtful.

You cannot rely on these facts alone to further your career. You must still prepare and tell your stories. However, this kind of information does do a lot for you in building trust, credibility, and a reputation for being the kind of person others want to work with.

> *CAUTION:* *Remember that you can also circulate negative information about yourself through your casual words and actions. If you tell how you got even with a noisy neighbor, you are demonstrating that you are vengeful. If you reveal a confidence of a coworker, you are saying that you cannot be trusted. If you don't respond to a customer because it is not your responsibility, you come across as lacking accountability.*

Blow Your Horn Outside Work, Too

You obviously want to use professional associations and networks as opportunities to blow your horn, but do not limit yourself to professional occasions. You never know when it might be useful for someone to know something about you. Neighborhood parties, children's soccer games, and other social occasions are also opportunities for self-promotion.

CAUTION: You must be extremely careful that your stories and accounts fit naturally into the conversation. Also, do not obviously broach a subject solely because you want to create an opportunity to talk about yourself. If someone is talking about having trouble with her boss at work and you have successfully resolved a similar situation, then of course tell her about it. However, you do not ask her how things are going at work to provide you with an excuse to tell her what you are doing.

Reality Check: How Are You Doing?

To assess whether you are ready to strategically engage in self-promotion, ask yourself the following questions:

+ What are my career goals?

+ What strengths and attributes recommend me for the direction I have chosen?

+ What stories, personal and professional, demonstrate those strengths and attributes?

+ Where do I want to go next (for example, a promotion, a new assignment, or skill development)?

+ Are there any people in particular whom I want to be aware of what I can do?

    ✧ Why have I selected those people?

    ✧ Do I have access to them directly?

    ✧ Who do I know that has access to them?

    ✧ How might I gain access to them?

+ Who in the company is doing what I am doing or what I want to be doing?

  ⟡ What do I want to learn from them?

  ⟡ How can I initiate contact?

+ Who in the company might benefit from my expertise or past experience?

+ Who can I support by singing their praises? What do I want to say about them?

+ Who can I ask to spread the word about me? What do I want them to say? Who do I want them to say it to?

KEEP SIGHT OF THE SHORE

If You Think You Can Walk on Water, You Are Likely to Drown

It is a given that self-confidence is essential to achieving success in any realm, and this most certainly holds true in the world of work. Confidence is what keeps you going in the face of challenges. It motivates and helps you stay at the top of your game. You gain credibility with others when they sense you have confidence in yourself. Conversely, if you don't have faith in your own abilities, you can be sure that no one else will.

Having said that, remember that confidence does not automatically translate to, nor is it a substitute for, competence. Although this might seem blatantly obvious, far too many people have stumbled because they saw the two as one and the same.

How does this happen? People overdose on confidence. There is a fine line between confidence and overconfidence, and it is not always easy to distinguish between the two. An inflated sense of your knowledge and abilities, if unchecked, can lead you to places that you'll wish you had never gone.

As your confidence in your abilities rightfully grows with your achievements, it takes on a life of its own. You might start to feel like you can do anything—and that is not always going to be the case. It's easy to overestimate your capacities based on what you have accomplished in the past, what others expect of you, or underestimating the challenges of a new project or initiative. Then there's always the added enticement of the value placed on stretching and taking risks.

Overconfidence can undermine your success just as easily as the lack of it. The first step in avoiding this pitfall is to be mindful of the possibility that you could easily get into situations in which you cannot meet all of the expectations.

Identify What's Different

Certainly, when your successes mount in any particular area, your confidence in your abilities grows right along with them. This is how it should be. However, although situations might appear similar on the surface, the details vary. Sometimes those details can make a big difference in the ultimate outcome.

> *Pat was senior human resources executive with a strong background in corporate restructuring and re-staffing (in which employees bid for all positions whose job descriptions are changed by virtue of the restructure; this usually impacts 90 percent of employees and results in some people not having a place in the new organization).*

> *In the planning stages of such an initiative, she convinced the senior team that her department could facilitate the effort and avoid the expense of an outside consultant. Pat was well-versed in the technical ins and outs of the process and its documentation requirements. She assured the executive team that in her previous projects her employers had never experienced successful litigation against them. She was certain that she could guarantee a smooth process and successful outcome.*

> *The re-staffing stretched over many months. As it cascaded down to supervisors and individual contributors, an already low level of trust exploded into a formidable problem. There was significant attrition as many top performers elected not to participate and left the company.*

Pat had failed to take into account this lack of trust in senior man-
agement and how internal facilitation of the process would exacerbate
it. Consequently, although the company had saved considerable con-
sultant expenses, it ultimately lost a great deal due to the exodus of
top talent.

In Pat's case, her previous successes took place in cultures that could better tolerate the disruption of a restructure. She had failed to consider
that, although the process was the same, the company in which it was
taking place was very different. Pat was so focused on what was similar
about the present and past situations that she did not even ask herself
what might be different.

Know What Made You Successful Before

In order to know what to look at in assessing the similarities and differences between past successes and a new situation, you need to understand what contributed to and supported your success in the former. Do
a careful analysis to ensure that you do not overlook critical factors that
accounted for your achieving the high-quality results that you did.

Identify the variables and conditions present during your efforts. Define
those factors that most contributed to success and those that might have
gotten in the way. Review your decisions, looking at the forks in the
road and why you decided on one particular course of action over
another. Be sure to take stock of what you might have done better or
differently. Review the homeruns and the near misses.

Such an inventory will serve you well when a similar situation comes
along. It will help you determine the probability that the same critical
factors that contributed to past successes will or will not influence the
outcome in the current situation. The list will guide you to understand
what you know, what you don't know, and what you need to find out.
It will help you determine when there are circumstances and conditions
that might hinder you, so that you can decide whether you can overcome them. The list will give you critical information by which to
determine the best course of action.

Know What You Do Well

In addition to knowing the circumstances that contributed to past successes, take stock of the skills and talents you brought to the table. You might not always be aware of *specifically* what you did that contributed to the success of any endeavor. You have certain skills, talents, and abilities that are second nature—so much so that you might not even be aware of what they are. Even if you know you are strong in an area, you might not understand exactly what you do that makes you so good.

A stellar facilitator might not be able to account for everything he or she does and does not do that makes him or her so good. A great salesperson is not necessarily aware of all the factors that make her or him so successful.

When you know that you shine at something, make sure you understand *why* you do. If you cannot identify what it is that accounts for your superior skill, get feedback to that effect. It might be uncomfortable to ask another person what you do that makes you so good at something, but it is critical information to have. It is important to know exactly *why* you are successful at some things because you can then deliberately do more of it and improve upon what you already do well.

At times, however, the same behavior that contributed to your success in past situations will not be helpful in the current one. For example, your ability to facilitate a group to consensus will not serve you in a situation that calls for you to make tough decisions alone in order to be successful. If your superior ability to analyze and understand complex data requires ample time to study it, you will not shine in circumstances when sufficient time is not available.

Know What You Don't Do Well

Conversely, you might have weaknesses or gaps that were inconsequential in a previous situation that can trip you up in the new one. Perhaps the new situation calls for skills that you didn't need in the past. You want to be sure that you know upfront what will be required of you so that if you are deficient in a necessary skill, you can compensate for what you lack.

If a new situation requires good organizational skills and that is not your strong suit, take preemptive action so that you can succeed. You might want to engage the support of someone with those skills, either to participate or to coach you along the way. If you are not well-versed in a software program that will be used, bring yourself up to speed or defer to someone who is proficient.

Do a Reality Check

It is not uncommon for people to overestimate what they can do or to be unaware of what they cannot do. This is where feedback becomes of ultimate importance.

In Secret 4, we talked about how to obtain honest feedback, and the beginning of a new undertaking is a critical time to do so. If you will be trying an untested skill or navigating new territory, set up feedback sources from the beginning. If you are certain that you possess the skills and qualities necessary for success, ask yourself why you are so sure. If honest, reliable feedback is not part of the answer to that question, validate that you indeed have the strengths that you think you have.

Action Items

❏ Look back on a past project that went well and account for the reasons why. Assess what skills and knowledge you contributed and identify the circumstances that helped or hindered. Note what others did to make it successful. Think of what could you have done differently or better.

❏ Make a list of those things you do well and exactly what contributes to your excelling in those particular areas. Make a list of areas where you are weak.

❏ Validate your assessments by seeking input from others who are in a position to offer meaningful feedback.

If You Think You Can Do Something in Your Sleep—Don't!

You probably have skills and expertise that, due to innate ability and years of experience, come extremely easily to you. You can do them almost without thinking. Be careful. It is just that fact that can lead to trouble. It is possible to be overconfident, even if you are a recognized genius at something.

You can get careless and overlook something, or you might not pay the necessary attention to what you are doing while you are doing it. Perhaps you are not as meticulous in your preparation, or you take something for granted that should be double-checked. It's during the times when you are absolutely certain that you have the situation well under control that you want to be extra diligent to ensure that you are right.

Don't procrastinate getting started on a task or project because you anticipate that it will be easy, or because you've done it so many times before. You never know when something unexpected will pop up. Make sure that you give yourself as much time as you would if the activity were new to you, and follow up in the same manner as you would if you were not so confident of the outcome.

Ignore These Thoughts!

If you find these thoughts running through your mind, don't listen to them!

+ "This spreadsheet will be a piece of cake. I won't worry about it until Monday morning."

+ "I've written so many programs like this, debugging it won't hold any surprises."

+ "The last meeting at the Four Seasons went so well, I don't need to get out there until the afternoon before."

Anticipate Problems

It's always a good idea to assess upfront everything that could possibly go wrong so that you can troubleshoot ahead of time if possible. When you are ultimately responsible for any important task or project, it's a good idea to go through a "what-if" analysis to anticipate and plan for any potential problems.

Often, you might be too close to the issue or too caught up in the details to identify what might trip you up. Check with others who have had similar projects to get the benefit of their experience and suggestions. Invite the participation of others and don't edit what you come up with. Make the list as long as possible. You can always disregard the items that you decide are too far out or over the top.

> *Josh was a change-management guru for an international management consulting company. He was charged with the development, design, and delivery of a program at multiple sites throughout the United States for an important Fortune 100 client. He accurately assessed that he had all the right stuff to do the job. His knowledge of the subject, instructional design skills, and training prowess made him more than equal to the task.*
>
> *The train-the-trainer session prior to the rollout was extremely well-received and Josh was confident that the training would be on target and consistent across sites. The training materials were reproduced at corporate headquarters in New York and scheduled to be shipped two days prior to the launch of the program.*
>
> *Oops. A surprise spring blizzard grounded the express delivery planes. Josh ended up sending the programs electronically to all the field offices, necessitating that they spend a frantic and sleepless weekend gathering the necessary materials and compiling them locally. The glitch was not apparent to the client but Josh's colleagues would long remember the frustration and angst that they considered unnecessary had Josh planned more carefully.*

Josh correctly assessed that he had the skills and knowledge necessary to deliver the best possible results and he planned carefully to allow sufficient time for material preparation and shipping. He just failed to consider the remote possibility of inclement weather. Of course, Josh could not be held responsible for the weather conditions. However, had the possibility of extreme weather been on his radar screen, he could have shipped the materials earlier and avoided the need for his colleagues to scramble in order to compensate for the problem.

Don't Promise What You Can't Control

When compiling the "what-if" list for any undertaking, pay special attention to those factors that are beyond your control. If important benchmarks depend on the actions and responses of others outside your purview, you might not have the necessary influence to guarantee that they will come through exactly as you want them to. Carefully evaluate the extent to which you can expect others to deliver as necessary.

If you have a long history with another person or outside organization and they have been reliable in the past, it's highly probable that they will continue to do so. If you have some kind of power because you have something that the other person wants, he or she will be more likely to come through as you need him or her to. If the other party has the same or higher stakes in the success of any endeavor, you can be more assured that they will do what is necessary to achieve it. You can count more on cooperation if you are a valued customer of an entity that wants to keep your business.

However, when you have no history, power, or other good reason to be sure that a person or organization will perform optimally as required, be circumspect as to the extent to which you rely on them. Leave room in your estimation of time frames in case the person is late in delivering or the work is substandard and in need of polishing.

> *Elaine was the main contractor for a highly publicized, state-of-the-art office park construction project. The bidding was quite competitive and her firm was selected based on cost and aggressive time projections for completion. The contract included cost-per-day fees should the project extend beyond the date promised, with financial rewards for finishing ahead of schedule.*

Elaine was convinced that the time frames were totally doable. Her projections allowed more than ample leeway for subcontractor delays and for any glitches resulting from the government regulatory approval process. She had conferred extensively with the agencies involved before making her estimations and was assured that her pre dictions were more than realistic. She guaranteed the client and her firm that she could manage the project to a timely, if not early, completion.

What no one anticipated was a shakeup in the municipal building department. The subsequent political posturing and in-fighting considerably delayed the approval of the civil, architectural, and structural plans. This led to further setbacks and significant delays, costing the firm a good deal of money and leaving them with a very unhappy client.

Manage Expectations

Once you have made a realistic assessment of possible roadblocks and you are clear about what factors are under your control and those that are not, be sure to consider these issues when you are making commitments to customers and stakeholders. It is better to underpromise, and then delight them, than it is to be overly optimistic and disappoint.

In Elaine's case, the players in the building department were not affected one way or another by when the project was completed, nor did Ellen have any compelling power over them. Thus, their political agenda took precedence over her business priorities. She could have mitigated the damages by making it clear to her client from the beginning that she could not absolutely guarantee the conduct of the regulatory agencies. Had she not put so much stock in the promises of the building department, she could have prepared the client for unforeseen contingencies. Had she done so, the client and her firm would not have been so surprised at the delays, nor would they have held Elaine accountable for them.

In the beginning of any important undertaking, refer to your "what-if" list to clearly lay out what you can promise without reservation and what depends on circumstances and other people beyond your own control. Paint the best possible scenario, clarifying those conditions that might impede progress or undercut results. Then, make sure that everyone is informed when everything is going as anticipated and when you encounter speed bumps and roadblocks. Let them know of the possible impact and exactly what you are doing to address the situation and facilitate the best outcome.

Pay Close Attention to the Details

Don't underestimate the power of small snafus to cause big problems. The little stuff can trip you up just as easily as the big stuff, so pay equal attention to it. Stories abound about small oversights that have led to disasters. For example, an important project proposal to an express delivery company was sent overnight via a competitor. In another instance, a marketing manager asked her assistant to book a flight for a critical presentation in Portland, and upon arriving at the airport discovered her e-ticket was for Oregon when she was expected in Maine.

Pay attention to even the smallest details while there is still time to correct for them. As you are walking out the door to meet an important client is no time to discover a stain on your clothes. An unanticipated traffic jam can make you late for a meeting that you are scheduled to conduct. When minor things go wrong, even if you manage to overcome them, they put you under stress and the adrenaline starts flowing. There is not always time to recover sufficiently so that your effectiveness does not suffer.

If you are driving somewhere for the first time, do a trial run to make sure that you know exactly how to get there. Neither MapQuest nor your GPS will tell you about road construction or limited parking. Complete important documents well ahead of the deadline to give you ample time and fresh eyes to make sure there are no typos or grammatical errors. Triple-check numbers and spreadsheets. If you are traveling, leave yourself plenty of time to gather personal belongings and professional materials necessary for a successful trip.

Know That You Might Not Know

When you are stretching your limits and doing something for the first time, you can probably assume that there are things you don't know. Check with people who have experience in what for you is new territory and learn as much as you can from them. Find out what worked and what didn't work. Ask what the potential pitfalls might be and how to recognize them. Inquire about their biggest mistakes and greatest triumphs, and what accounted for them. Gain permission to check in along the way for their feedback and advice.

Even when something is not new to you, allow for the possibility that you might be missing something or operating on insufficient information. If you are to avoid being blindsided, it is important to double-check for any suppositions that might have holes in them or be based on miscalculations. Get the input of others who are involved or have experience in that area. It is always useful to have a sounding board—someone who will call it like he or she sees it and not just tell you what you want to hear.

Action Items

❏ Look at what must go right for an important task or project to be successful and make a list of possible problems or obstacles.

❏ Identify aspects that are not under your control and list ideas of how best to deal with them.

❏ List the important and minor details that must be attended to.

Get Everyone on the Same Page...

When you find yourself in a situation in which your success requires collaboration and cooperation with others within your own organization, don't assume you can count on them simply because you are the lead. Pay attention upfront to creating an environment in which everyone is aligned around a common goal and committed to its achievement. Focus on the outcome and create individual and group accountability to minimize political posturing and in-fighting that can undermine the quality of the results. Make sure that there are open channels of communication and a continuing feedback loop.

...Then Invite Disagreement

Having said that, you do not want everyone to see eye-to-eye on everything and you must be careful not to set the expectation that they should. It is through disagreement and debate that you arrive at the best solutions and highest-quality results. You do not want people to be silent when they have questions or disagree with something for fear of appearing less than knowledgeable or not being regarded as a team player.

Make sure that people feel free to voice objections and differences of opinion from the very beginning. If there is no permission to do so, you cheat yourself out of valuable insights and also leave yourself open to sabotage as the project progresses. Assume that some disagreement is not only inevitable, but necessary, to achieving the best results, and that it is better to directly address it than to ignore it or sweep it under the carpet.

Look for and Invite "Bad News"

In every work situation there will be minor problems, delays, and possibly challenging roadblocks. It is obvious that the only way to overcome any difficulties is to know about them so that you can take corrective action. Therefore, you must guard against overlooking or disregarding important information.

Know that there is a natural tendency in everyone to see only those things that fit with a preconceived notion of how things ought to be or how you want them to be, thus leaving you vulnerable to disregarding or dismissing important signals that things are awry.

> *Gary was the sales rep for a large office-supply company with several large corporate accounts. He had dealt with Tim, his biggest client, for several years and had a very strong relationship with him. During a*

time when Tim was experiencing some significant personal problems, Gary noticed that he was canceling appointments and not returning e-mails. Gary attributed this to Tim's personal life and thought nothing of it until Tim informed him that the company was switching to another vendor.

Gary might have been able to turn around the situation had he placed the necessary importance on, and responded to, the signals that something might be amiss. It wasn't unreasonable for him to conclude that Tim's distance was due to his personal situation; however, he could have validated his assumption.

He should have left a simple voice-mail or e-mail message acknowledging that Tim was less available than usual and asked whether there were any problems he did not know about. This would not have guaranteed a different outcome, but it would have at least given Tim an opening and Gary a shot at remedying whatever it was that caused Tim to select another vendor.

Be clear about what it will look like when things are going as they should, and be especially alert to when anything might be even a little off. It is always better to err on the side of caution than to erroneously disregard circumstances or information that can signal problems and ultimately undermine your success.

Just a few of the warning signs to be on the lookout for are the following:

+ Credible complaints from internal or external customers

+ Unexpected situations or things you have not seen before

+ A project not going as anticipated

+ A project going as anticipated, but largely due to luck

+ Constant revision of the project plan

+ Problems arising due to communication issues

Sometimes information or circumstances are open to several interpretations. In those cases, check yourself to make sure that you are not rationalizing it away or choosing a particular interpretation because it is the most desirable or convenient one. Get ideas from others about what else might be going on and then check them out.

> *CAUTION:* *Although you want to make sure that you don't disregard when a task or project is going a bit (or a lot) off course, you don't want to overreact to events or issues that are ultimately meaningless. Allow for some variation in the way things proceed and know that everything is not going to be perfect or exactly as planned. If you feel too close to the situation, enlist the perspective of others who you trust to be objective and supportive of your success. Know that if you second-guess everything, others will see you as lacking confidence in yourself and in them. You have to find the balance between when it's necessary to take corrective action and when you can overlook small blips on the radar screen.*

Sometimes you will not be in a position to keep on top of everything that occurs during the course of a project and will have to rely on others to monitor progress. Be sure to let them know at the outset what information you want from them, including problems and concerns. Tune their antennae to notice the kinds of things that are on your "what-if" list. Then, just like when you are receiving personal or professional feedback, be extremely careful not to shoot the messenger.

There may be times when the difficulty could have been anticipated or avoided. Even worse, the problem might be directly traceable to the careless error of the individual reporting it. Take a deep breath and make sure you do not respond emotionally or point out what he or she did wrong. At times the temptation to blame and critique is overwhelming, but *don't do it.* If you do, you are setting up a situation where you won't have future information vital to the success of your work.

If you cannot trust yourself to respond in a calm fashion, simply thank the individual and let this person know you appreciate her or his honesty. Tell her or him that you need to think about it for a while and you will get back in touch. Further, even if the individual bringing you the bad news is not responsible for the problem, you still do not want her or him to witness your emotional reaction. It can be uncomfortable and a deterrent to her or him coming to you in the future.

Be careful that in your efforts to calm yourself down, you don't vent to someone who might at a later time be in the same position as the person you are talking about. If you do, the person you are venting to will think twice before he or she ever comes to you with unwelcome news. Also, you don't want to share your frustration with anyone who might be tempted to relate your conversation to others. The safest thing to do if you need to shed your angst by talking about it is to select a trusted listener with no involvement or stake in the situation.

Own Up to Problems and Mistakes

When you do encounter problems or obstacles, admit them, own them, and do what you can to overcome them. Assuming you have done a good job of anticipating what might go wrong and informing customers and stakeholders ahead of time, there should be very few surprises. However, when there are mistakes, be upfront about them. Present issues calmly and address how you are managing them.

CAUTION: Do not run to customers and stakeholders with every glitch along the way. They need not be informed if the issue will not significantly affect the outcome, or if any damage can easily be rectified. At the same time, you need to be careful that they don't find out about something from another source that might lead them to believe that you are concealing important information from them. Use your best judgment in determining when to alert customers and stakeholders and when not to. You might want to get clear at the beginning of a project or task about what they want to be informed about and what they don't.

When letting people know of problems, be sure not to engage in finger pointing. Even if the issue is due to someone else's mistake or oversight, do not lay blame on that individual. If you are in charge, you are expected to take full responsibility for progress or the lack of it. Should another's name inadvertently slip into the discussion, take ownership of the problem. Say something like "I must not have clearly communicated to Sally what we were looking for. She will get me the information immediately and we can proceed with minimal delay."

Beware of the Henry Kissinger Effect

Just as you don't want to be overconfident about what you can do, neither do you want to overestimate the capabilities of others or be misled by their overconfidence in themselves. Henry Kissinger once said that the best thing about being a celebrity is that if you bore people, they think it's their fault. Indeed, once people have attained a certain level of achievement and stature, others tend to attribute all kinds of qualities to them which that person may or may not possess. We are then in jeopardy of giving them more credibility than is warranted in a given situation or inadvisably deferring to them in matters where there are differing viewpoints.

Every organization has its heroes and superstars. Usually, their reputations are well deserved, earned through excellent performance, strong expertise, and superior results. Such stature and credibility is likely the result of a long string of homeruns and wins. Quite rightly, the ability to influence grows with each mounting success. However, no one is infallible and it can be a mistake to be influenced solely on the basis of another's reputation or expertise.

> *Gail was a new instructional designer for a farm-equipment manufacturing company. Her first major project was to develop a management training program based on a recently published book by a well-reputed consultant. He had been hired to provide executive coaching to the senior team and was held in high regard throughout the company. Gail was expected to use him as a resource to ensure the integrity of the program.*

She was confused about several concepts in the book. Despite dili-gently poring over the material, in her mind there were several dis-connects and inconsistencies. Unfortunately, conversations with the consultant did nothing to clear up things for her. Gail was frustrated by her inability to master these concepts as she considered herself to be quite bright and highly skilled.

Over time her confidence began to erode and she relied more and more on the consultant. As the project stumbled slowly along, Gail was reassigned to other duties and the program was handed over to a more senior designer. He later informed Gail that the problem was not with her, but rather with the book itself. Some of the premises were not well thought out or succinctly articulated. Gail had falsely concluded that since the consultant had written a book, his expertise trumped hers and she was the one who was lacking.

In the preceding example, Gail did not trust her own instincts and came to question her ability because she automatically assumed that the author/consultant, by virtue of his reputation and achievements, must be right. Even though she was eventually able to overcome her rocky start, Gail need not have risked her success with the company by calling so much attention to her struggles.

> *CAUTION: This does not mean that you recklessly challenge others or deliberately point out when someone might have gaps or flaws in their thinking process. Secret 3 addressed the importance of not making others wrong or relentlessly pur-suing your own perspective with no regard to its impact on others. Note that in order for Gail to complete her charge, she did not have to directly challenge the consultant. She could quietly go about bridging the gaps in his material without having to confront him or call attention to the fact that she was doing so.*

Trust in What You Know

Even if you are aware of the Henry Kissinger Effect, it is not always easy to determine whether you are under its influence. The first step in doing so is to have realistic confidence in your own skills, abilities, and knowledge.

When something seems off to you, or you have difficulty grasping a concept, a well-founded trust in yourself is essential in determining how to proceed. Instead of automatically assuming that you are wrong and another is right, take a break from the situation. Think things through again and observe the issues with fresh eyes. Describe the circumstances objectively to a trusted colleague with similar experience and get her or his perspective and input.

In addition, take into consideration what motives you might have in unquestioningly deferring to another. When in the presence of stardom, you might not want to risk being seen as less competent than the other, or even worse, appear to be stupid. You also might want to win his or her favor and fear that challenging him or her might be experienced as an affront. If any of these motives—or motives like them—accounts for your choices, you might want to think twice (or three times)! Let the situation dictate the best course of action, not the other person's opinion of you.

The Henry Kissinger Effect Works Both Ways

You can also find yourself in situations where others are blinded by your star-shine. It does not ultimately serve you if you are given deference because of it. Beware of being so humble that you fail to recognize when this is occurring, or so flattered that you, too, believe you are infallible. When you notice that people tend to consistently follow your lead, adopt your perspective, and acquiesce to your way of doing things, stop and ask yourself why this is occurring.

If it's happening because people think you know more than they do and are smarter or more competent than they are, don't jump to the conclusion that they must be correct every time. It is important to remember that the possibility always exists that you are wrong, have insufficient information, or have failed to take something important into account. If you bask in your own stardom and believe your own press too fervently, you could be headed in a direction you don't want to go.

If indeed others have you on a pedestal, you have to make a concerted effort to climb down to a place where everyone is playing on an even field. Actively solicit their input. Ask not only what others think, but *why* they see things as they do. Listen carefully for something you might have failed to take into account. Listen for the reasons why their ideas are sound and well thought out and then say so. If possible, yield to their perspective if it will work as well—or almost as well—as yours.

Just as I talked about receiving bad news and feedback in such a way as to ensure that people will continue to give it to you, you want to do the same thing with differing points of view. Sometimes, even when you are the expert and have sound ideas, others' input can make a good thing better. Even if a particular approach or solution has worked well in the past, be open to other ways of doing things that might be equally—or more—effective.

Request that people play devil's advocate to all ideas, especially those that everyone seems to easily agree upon. By endorsing this kind of dialogue, you are taking out insurance against "group think" and the Henry Kissinger Effect.

Take Advantage of All Learning Opportunities

When you have the occasion to read a new book, attend a workshop, or listen to a speaker, don't decline because you think you won't learn anything new. Time is precious and sometimes it seems a waste of it to focus on something about which you are already competent and confident. However, it is best to assume that there is always something new to learn—because there usually is.

Reality Check: How Are You Doing?

If you are working on an important task or project, or are about to start on one, use the following questions as a measure of how effectively you have assessed the situation in order to safeguard against costly mistakes.

If you think you know the answer to a question, ask your self *how you know.* You want to be sure you are not operating on assumptions, but rather, on valid information from your own observations or a trusted source. If for any reason you are in doubt about an answer, double-check to confirm your perception.

This is by all means not a comprehensive list of everything you need to know, nor is it implied that every question is relevant to your particular situation. However, the exercise is useful as a litmus test to indicate whether you are on the right track.

+ What is the same and what is different about the current situation as compared to past ones where I have been successful?

+ What are the strengths that I bring to the task or project? What are the weaknesses and how will I manage them?

+ What problems or roadblocks might possibly get in the way of my success? How can I troubleshoot them ahead of time? How will I manage them if I cannot?

+ What is under my control and what is not?

+ What do my customers and stakeholders expect? Are their expectations realistic? What have I communicated about what is and what is not under my control?

+ What details—major and minor—must be attended to?

+ Does everyone on the team have the same understanding of the desired outcome and what it takes to achieve it? Who is accountable for what? How are they held accountable? Is there open and honest communication, with permission to voice differing points of view and opinions?

✦ What are some specific signs of trouble or problems for which I should be on the alert?

✦ Am I giving an individual or individual(s) credit for knowledge or skill based only on reputation or assumption? How can I validate that they have it?

✦ Might others be giving me credit that is unwarranted? If so, what can I do about it?

INDEX